TAROT INSTINCT

INTERPRETING THE TAROT

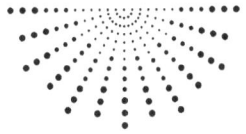

LYDIA STRAUB

Tarot Instinct V2
Interpreting the Tarot

Copyright 2021 Lydia Straub
lydiastraub@outlook.com
Instagram: @tarotlydia
Facebook: Lydia Straub

All rights reserved. This book or parts thereof may not be reproduced in any form, stored in any retrieval system, or transmitted in any form by any means—electronic, mechanical, photocopy, recording, or otherwise—without prior written permission of the publisher

ISBN: 978-1-7772077-3-1

Tarot images reproduced from copyright free images. All other images are copyright protected purchased for use by the author. Reproduction without permission is forbidden.

CONTENTS

Part I
OVERVIEW

1. THE FOOL ENCOUNTERS THE WORLD	3
2. LEARNING THE TAROT CARDS	7
Practice	8
Getting Started	9
Decks	10
Shuffling	11
Reversals	12
Significator	13
Fortune Telling	14
Death	14
Negativity	15
3. TAROT SPREADS	16

Part II
THE MAJOR ARCANA

1. THE FOOL	27
Number 0 Symbolism	31
Chakra	33
Correspondence	34
Reading Card Placement	34
Yes / No Key Interpretation	35
Keywords	35
2. THE MAGICIAN	36
Number 1 Symbolism	39
Chakra	41
Correspondence	42
Reading Card Placement	42
Yes / No Key Interpretation	43
Keywords	43

3. THE HIGH PRIESTESS	44
Number 2 Symbolism	46
Chakra	48
Correspondences	49
Reading Card Placement	49
Yes / No Key Interpretation	50
Keywords	50
4. THE EMPRESS	51
Number 3 Symbolism	54
Chakra	57
Correspondences	58
Reading Card Placement	58
Yes / No Key Interpretation	59
Keywords	59
5. THE EMPEROR	60
Number 4 Symbolism	62
Chakra	64
Correspondences	65
Reading Card Placement	65
Yes / No Key Interpretation	66
Keywords	66
6. THE HIEROPHANT	67
Number 5 Symbolism	69
Chakra	71
Correspondences	72
Reading Card Placement	72
Yes / No Interpretation	73
Keywords	74
7. THE LOVERS	75
Number 6 Symbolism	78
Chakra	80
Correspondences	81
Reading Card Placement	81
Yes / No Key Interpretation	82
Keywords	82
8. THE CHARIOT	83
Number 7 Symbolism	85
Chakra	87

Correspondences	88
Reading Card Placement	88
Yes / No Key Interpretation	89
Keywords	89
9. STRENGTH	90
Number 8 Symbolism	92
Chakra	94
Correspondence	95
Reading Card Placement	95
Yes / No Key Interpretation	96
Keywords	96
10. THE HERMIT	97
Number 9 Symbolism	100
Chakra	102
Correspondence	103
Reading Card Placement	103
Yes / No Key Interpretation	104
Keywords	104
11. THE WHEEL OF FORTUNE	105
Number 10 Symbolism	107
Chakra	109
Correspondences	110
Yes / No Key Interpretation	111
Keywords	111
12. JUSTICE	112
Number 11 Symbolism	114
Chakra	116
Correspondence	117
Reading Card Placement	117
Yes / No Key Interpretation	118
Keywords	118
13. HANGED MAN	119
Number 12 Symbolism	121
Chakra	123
Correspondences	123
Reading Card Placement	124
Yes / No Key Interpretation	125
Keywords	125

14. DEATH	126
Number 13 Symbolism	128
Chakra	130
Correspondences	131
Reading Card Placement	131
Yes / No Key Interpretation	132
Keywords	132
15. TEMPERANCE	133
Number 14 Symbolism	135
Chakra	137
Correspondence	138
Reading Card Placement	138
Yes / No Key Interpretation	139
Keywords	139
16. THE DEVIL	140
Number 15 Symbolism	142
Chakra	144
Correspondence	145
Reading Card Placement	145
Yes / No Key Interpretation	146
Keywords	147
17. THE TOWER	148
Number 16 Symbolism	150
Chakra	152
Correspondences	153
Reading Card Placement	153
Yes / No Key Interpretation	154
Keywords	154
18. THE STAR	155
Number 17 Symbolism	157
Chakra	159
Correspondences	160
Reading Card Placement	160
Yes / No Key Interpretation	161
Keywords	161
19. THE MOON	162
Number 18 Symbolism	164
Chakra	166

Correspondences	166
Reading Card Placement	167
Yes / No Key Interpretation	168
Keywords	168
20. THE SUN	169
Number 19 Symbolism	171
Chakra	173
Correspondences	174
Reading Card Placement	174
Yes / No Key Interpretation	175
Keywords	175
21. JUDGEMENT	176
Number 20 Symbolism	178
Chakra	180
Correspondences	181
Reading Card Placement	181
Yes / No Key Interpretation	182
Keywords	182
22. THE WORLD	183
Number 21 Symbolism	185
Chakra	187
Correspondences	188
Reading Card Placement	188
Yes / No Key Interpretation	189
Keywords	189

Part III
THE MINOR ARCANA

1. WANDS	193
2. CUPS	208
3. SWORDS	223
4. PENTACLES	238

Part IV
MULTIPLE CARDS

1. ACES	255
2. TWOS	257
3. THREES	260

4. FOURS	262
5. FIVES	264
6. SIXES	266
7. SEVENS	268
8. EIGHTS	270
9. NINES	272
10. TENS	274
11. PAGES	276
12. KNIGHTS	278
13. QUEENS	280
14. KINGS	282
Notes	285
About the Author	287

PART I
OVERVIEW

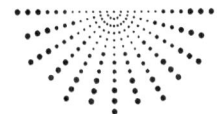

"The true Tarot is symbolism: it speaks a language that arises from the collective mind of Man."

Eden Gray

1
THE FOOL ENCOUNTERS THE WORLD

The Tarot cards are a mystical symbolism of our world. Beautiful and inspiring they help us find our way through the weeds of our life to the truth.

However, the Tarot is not a fortune telling deck. It will not predict your future, nor tell you things that are unknown. Instead, it is a guide to your inner soul, your unconscious needs, your 'gut' feelings and desires. Using the Tarot allows us to focus on what we truly want to achieve, and which processes we will use to get there.

According to Jung, it does this through psychological images that connect with you, pulling out those hidden things that need to be known. Individual cards speak to you, while combinations of the cards create strong possible stories for you to run through. "The cards," said Jung, "combine in certain ways, and the different combinations correspond to the playful development of mankind."

"Psychoanalysts have looked with respect upon the symbols and their connection with the subconscious activities of the human psyche. Among those who have taken cognizance of the Tarot are T. S. Eliot, in The Waste Land; Charles Williams, in The Greater Trumps; William Lindsay Gresham, in Nightmare Alley; and P. D. Ouspensky, in A New Model of the Universe. A. E., the famous Irish poet, belonged to the Order of the Golden Dawn, and the poet W. B. Yeats was also a member of a secret order that dealt with the Tarot's occult traditions. The followers of the famous psychoanalyst C. G. Jung see symbols in the cards that relate to the archetypes of the collective unconscious."[1]

The images in the Tarot are archetypal. An archetype is a fundamental pattern of inborn thought and found deep in the subconscious mind. Archetypes are not gender specific, even if the image indicates a gender. Nor do they represent specific cultures. Gender labels are created by you and society. The best way to use the Tarot is to be gender and culture non-specific, allowing any image to represent what your unconscious is seeking to reveal to you in the moment. Archetypes can represent, mother, child, death and others. When viewing a Tarot card, do not assume that a King for instance, is always a male or a Queen always a female. We are complex beings, made up of part female, part male, somewhat introvert, somewhat extrovert, strong and weak components. Which is why it is absurd to hate based on any identification because, in fact, you are hating a piece of yourself.

Eden Gray states in *A Complete Guide To The Tarot*, "A study of the cards also discloses a close relationship to the Kabalistic lore of the ancient Hebrews. In short, there can be no doubt that whoever actually invented the Tarot knew ancient religions and philosophies and embodied many of their symbols in the cards."[2] This book considers the relationship between the Tarot, Kabbalah, Chakras, the I Ching and Astrology, as all seem to be inter-related and enhance the other.

At times the cards may seem to predict the future, while in fact you are simply working through what your unconscious has revealed to you. In a twisted way, they do predict your future, because you are following a path you already, unconsciously, laid out for yourself.

The Tarot deck traces The Fool's Journey through life, with all the accomplishments, skill development, setbacks, love, and loss that occur in a normal life. As a metaphor for any of the human experiences of the world, The Fool's Journey shows us our own personal path as we wind our way down the road. The Fool travels through the Tarot, meeting the archetypes of the Major Arcana, learning and growing from his encounters. The journey mirrors our travels, as we make our way in life, stumbling, learning, loving, occasionally falling flat on our face. The Fool can teach us much, and through his journey, we may learn the pitfalls to avoid and the joy that can be generated from choosing one particular path over the other.

At any point in time, your life may be illustrated through a Tarot card, as it shows the processes in play and made known through the card's placements in a layout. Each card in the Major Arcana creates a story, indicating a specific focus that you need to pay attention to: spirituality, learning, health, relationships or career. These are your life lessons which you can choose to take on or ignore. However, if you ignore them, the lessons will return, sometimes in a different format, with different individuals.

The Major Arcana cards are the cards that don't leave until you have completed the associated learning. The Minor Arcana are cards that represent your experiences and situations; cards which you can move and change. By responding differently or taking a different action you can shift the minor arcana cards.

When you see the illustrated card (or cards), it clears the mind, bringing to surface all your unconscious thoughts and actions. With this knowledge exposed, you can make better decisions. Decisions that aid to clear away misunderstandings or any chaos currently surrounding your life.

The Tarot gives you the gift of a path to take at that moment. It does not tell you to take that path, only you can make that decision.

The Tarot moves, because you, and the world around you, move and change. What was shown in the Tarot yesterday, may not bring the same ideas today. The Tarot is simply a reflection of you and your inner self. When you view a Tarot layout, you are, in essence, looking at your own advice. Taking your own advice, as given to you in the Tarot layout, creates a flow in your life that moves you along the path. And the next Tarot reading will illustrate the changes and shifts that have occurred since the previous reading. These shifts may not be visible or appear in a concrete form. The shifts may occur inside you. Your attitude, your focus, your self-esteem may change. Which over time, may change your physical world as well.

The Tarot doesn't predict or force, it only pulls from you what you already know and sense about your world. If you don't follow the advice in the original layout, the cards will change with yet a different layout, as you've chosen a different path.

In the first leg of this journey, the Fool begins to encounter challenges which upset and confound him. After the stillness and mindfulness of the learning, his new-found sense of peace is disturbed, and The Fool must find ways of putting what he has learned into practice. The Fool thinks he has laid his ego aside and feels he can deal with these challenges. Thus, The Fool's ego begins to take charge once more. Of course, the The Fool is unable to recognize that he cannot control all things and ties himself in knots, causing great distress to the poor Fool.

Eventually, The Fool realizes that he can use the teachings of the Hermit to understand. Once again, he calms the ego and becomes still in the present, existing at the center of the Wheel. Allowing events to unfold as they will, The Fool begins to learn that the answers needed will come. He simply needs to stop chasing the answers he *wants* to hear and wait for the truth. The Fool remembers we are all one, and the Universe is one great entity, forever changing, eternally the same.

The cards depicted in this book are the Rider deck, with illustrations by Patricia Coleman. At this time, the Rider deck is the only copyright free deck. It was used by A. E. Waite in his book The Pictorial Key to the Tarot (1910), with later updates. The deck is considered the classic standard.

2

LEARNING THE TAROT CARDS

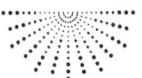

When learning the Tarot, the goal is to become an instinctual story teller. The cards are laid out before you and you must weave a story that tells of a compelling path so the seeker's unconscious begins to reveal itself. At first you will need to check the meanings of cards but as you gain experience and confidence, you will not only remember the traditional meanings, you will also begin to grasp the overall understanding in your 'gut'. This will allow you to speak to the cards with confidence, knowing that a card may have one meaning in this layout and a slightly different meaning in another layout. The stories vary as the seeker's life changes and flows into different rivers.

There are different categories that users of the Tarot belong to:

- The seeker who goes to professional Tarot readers for assistance and guidance
- A person who learns the Tarot but only uses the cards occasionally. Often, this individual will use the single card method, pulling a Tarot card out to gain insight into their day or a particular situation

- An individual who learns the Tarot and uses the cards frequently to consult for guidance but only for themselves
- An individual who consults for themselves and also for friends and family members with no charge
- A professional Tarot reader, who consults for money. Usually, this person has great intuitive skills and a deep understanding of the Tarot

Regardless of the category you belong to, the Tarot asks that you work within moral and ethical boundaries. Never use the cards or a reading for a negative intention.

PRACTICE

Like any other skill, the Tarot takes practice. To learn the Tarot, you must commit to using it daily so that your knowledge and intuition grows. If you wish to only learn enough to gain a deeper understanding of what your professional reader is telling you, then practice may not be required. Instead, you can take a picture of the layout and once home, consult this book or a website to gain a deeper understanding of what the reader has discussed with you.

Any other use of the Tarot takes practice. There is no easy path to the magic of knowledge. As your intuition and understanding of the inter-relationships between the cards grows, it may at times feel like magic. You can feel that you've developed another intuitive sense. And in some ways you will, for the practice you do brings with it the gradual dawning of intuition. The reality is intuition can be developed: it is a strength that comes from practice. Some of those with a more fully developed intuition may experience an easier time learning the cards, but they still must practice using that intuition with the Tarot.

As a beginner, you will be consulting this book constantly for explanations of the various cards. When your knowledge base is deeper, you will slowly gain confidence in your understanding until one day you realize it is a rare time that you have to consult a book or website. That is a time of celebration!

GETTING STARTED

Luckily, getting started is simple:

- Read this book thoroughly. Understand the introduction chapters including the difference between the Major and Minor arcana. Know how to prepare the deck and shuffle. Decide if you will use reversals while you learn. (It is recommended that you don't but use your instincts to decide)
- Choose your deck. Use only one deck while you are learning. Divide your cards into the Major Arcana and Minor Arcana
- Use the Major Arcana only first. Prepare your deck and shuffle as described below
- Each day layout a spread for yourself
- Start with pulling one card only
- Move to the three-card spread for a few weeks. Ask yourself, 'What is the story these 3 cards are telling?'
- Use the Celtic Cross spread to increase your skill
- Read the description of each card you pull. Take the time to look at the illustration, examining it for the symbolism, colors and details
- Keep a journal of your readings. Make comments on the cards. Which cards pull you to them when you are asking a specific question or dealing with an issue? Which cards are you tempted to ignore or dismiss? What does that mean - are you avoiding something or just have a strong gut feeling that other cards are more important? Are your readings shifting? If you do a daily reading are you finding a flow to the readings?
- When you feel comfortable with the Major Arcana, add in the Minor Arcana cards
- Focus on the story the cards are telling you. Look for relationships between the cards depending on their position. It will be a while before you can comfortably read a Tarot

layout without consulting a book, but hang in there. That day does come!

DECKS

There are currently, at a minimum, over 100 Tarot decks. Each year brings new ones developed by artists and seers with new outlooks on the Tarot. This book uses the original Waite/Coleman deck to illustrate the cards. The deck is readily available in bookstores and online. The symbolism is clear and easy to learn. It is recommended that you chose one deck to learn on and stick with it until you feel comfortable that you understand the underlying meaning of each of the cards. At that point you can add in additional decks that pull you to them.

Deciding on a deck is an adventure. You may choose the classic Waite/Coleman deck, the most popular deck. Or you may be drawn to another deck. Rather than buy your first deck online, it is suggested, if you can, that you go to a bookstore that carries the decks. There you can touch them to see if you feel any pull or sensation. You can look at the vibrant colors in real light and consider the symbolism reflected in each deck. A warning – it can be a bit overwhelming and a desire to buy 3 or 4 decks could arise. Let that go and pick one deck. That will be the deck that you learn on and use for the first while of your Tarot time.

Once you are comfortable with one deck, you can choose another to work with and learn the different symbolism. The reason for using only one deck is to ensure you understand the symbolism that is designed into each card. The art on each deck kind is different, and while the meanings generally remain the same, the symbolism helps guide readers to the true meanings of the card. If you switch between decks while learning, you may miss some of the symbolism inherent in each card. That said, using different books or websites to explore meanings is helpful.

Sometimes you are gifted a Tarot deck. The universe has ways of letting you know it is time to learn the Tarot. Or, if you are already a reader, to use a new deck.

It is not uncommon for a Tarot reader to have at least 3 or 4 decks.

They choose the deck to use based on the question asked, their mood or an intuitive feeling that a particular deck is best for this seeker.

Once you've purchased your deck, unwrap it, and examine the cards. Slowly go through the deck, looking at each card. Don't try to decipher the meanings, just experience the cards. Sort them by different ways – suits, Major and Minor Arcana, the court cards, all Aces, etc. Your journey begins by becoming familiar with the deck.

Each day draw one card and read the meaning. Do this as a meditative task. First thing in the morning works well, or in the evening as a way to wind down your day. Although you will be working on larger layouts, learning your way through the deck by pulling one card a day will reinforce your efforts.

Store your deck carefully. Some wrap the deck in a piece of silk, others have a wooden box dedicated to their cards. It's not important what you store them in. It is just important that you recognize the cards as special and don't leave them lying around getting dusty and possibly losing a card or two. Some Tarot readers feel that the cards can be influenced by the atmosphere around it around them. So choose carefully where you store them.

SHUFFLING

The cards must be shuffled each time you use them and for each reading. Relax, close your eyes and tap into your intuition before you begin shuffling. The goal is for your energy to flow into the cards. Focus on the question at hand.

First, clear the cards before you begin the shuffling by knocking on the card decks, much as you'd knock on a door. This pushes out any previous energy left in the cards.

Then begin shuffling. The question often arises 'how long do I shuffle for?'. The answer is 'until it feels right'. The answer is vague but over time as you work with the cards, you will come to understand that it is the right answer. You will gain the ability to sense when the cards have been shuffled long enough.

Next, if not seeking an answer for yourself, hand the deck to the seeker. It is generally accepted that the seeker (the person asking the question for the reading) shuffles the cards. The reader may clear the deck first and provide an initial shuffle, but the seeker completes the shuffle, so their energy goes into the deck. Inform the seeker that they should relax and focus on the question they want answered while they are shuffling.

When the shuffle is complete ask the seeker to place the deck on the table in front of them. Then have the seeker split the deck into 3 piles, first lifting some of the cards from the top and placing those cards to the left. Then, lifting some more of the cards, and placing those to the right of the deck. The reader then picks up the left-side pile, places it on top of the middle pile, picks up the entire middle pile and places it on top of the right pile. The deck is now ready for the cards to be drawn and placed in the desired spread.

REVERSALS

Many Tarot readers use reversals in their readings. Reversals are when the card appears upside down instead of the designed upright way. In this book, it is chosen to use only upright cards and meanings.

Using only upright cards is sometimes a controversial choice, as some readers swear that reversed cards are necessary to obtain the full picture of the reading. Reversals can add another dimension to a Tarot consultation, but a reversed card can also confuse and add difficulty when first learning the Tarot. You have 78 cards to gain insight into the meanings of, and your goal should be to have deep knowledge not a surface understanding. Your knowledge should include the interactions between the cards and how a particular card's significance can shift, depending on where it appears in a layout.

Tarot readers rely on the images to spark their memory and give them insight. If a card is upside down, it becomes challenging to view and to let any particular piece of the card spark insight. Tarot card artwork is created to be viewed right side up, not upside down. Each image touches you differently in each individual reading. This allows for a fuller, more intuitive reading. You may find that reverse cards, rather than adding to your reading, stop your intuition's flow and your mind's grasp of what needs to be said to the seeker.

The purpose of reading the Tarot is to garner insight – either for yourself or for a seeker. The reading will provide a way forward, ongoing hope and a flow into the seeker's next steps. Reversed cards can stop this flow and cause the reading to go deeply into negative energy. You can, of course, discern negative aspects of a situation in an upright only layout. But the images on the cards will add a story and depth, allowing you to create energy that taps into your intuition and the seeker's unconscious. Some readers find that a reversed card blocks that intuitive energy, causing the reading to stall.

If you are a beginner to Tarot consultation, ignoring the reversals by turning them upright is often the best way to go. If you wish to learn the reversed meanings after achieving competence with the upright images, do so. You can test if adding reversals at that stage adds dimension to your readings, giving you more options in layouts and readings or if it reduces your intuitive relationship to the cards.

SIGNIFICATOR

A significator is a card chosen to represent the seeker in a reading. Some chose a card based on the seeker's astrological sign. Others study the cards and get a 'feel' as to which one best represents them at that moment. Some select a card based on the physical looks and age of the seeker although that can be a misrepresentation. Some readers chose the significator for their seeker, others will select 4 cards and let the seeker choose. For example, 4 queens or 4 Kings based on the readers feeling of the seeker.

A once common way of selecting a significator was to use Kings for older men, Queens for older women, Knights for young men and Pages for young women. You could extend this to the physical looks with Wands being for fair skinned, Cups for blonde or light brown hair, Swords for dark hair and eyes and Pentacles for dark skin and hair. This technique obviously has difficulties. Many do not identify as just male or female. Or a male may self-identify as female. A young person may have the wisdom of an elder and an older person hasn't matured as they should. The represented color of hair in the age of hair dye is meaningless. No one should be slotted into a category based on their skin color. For all these reasons it is recommended not to use this method to select a significator. Instead, consider the personalities of the cards.

It is a personal choice whether the reader uses a significator or not. Some readers find it helps both them and the seeker remain focused on who the subject of the reading. Others find it makes no difference to the reading. Rather than help, it puts the emphasis on the meaning of the card chosen to be a significator, rather than the cards drawn and placed in the spread in regards to the question asked of the cards.

If you chose to use a significator, chose it before you start the reading, pulling the card from the deck and laying it out before you shuffle the deck. Usually, the significator is placed in Card 1 position of the spread and then Card 1 is placed over it.

FORTUNE TELLING

When doing a reading for a seeker always remind them you are not predicting their future. Rather, you are pulling their unconscious into the daylight, allowing them to see the hidden patterns at play in their life.

Remind them that nothing is in stone. If they don't like the outcome, they can change it by changing their actions or beliefs. The reading is in the hands of the seeker and is not fated. Each card is guiding them to a place of understanding where they can control their emotions, plans and energy to create the best possible outcome.

DEATH

There is no card in the Tarot that predicts the seeker's or the death of someone near to them. There is a card in the Major Arcana called Death. But as you will learn, this card represents change or leaving things behind to procure a new life.

Sometimes the 10 of Swords is called the death card, mainly because of the symbolism on the card. But that too is a myth.

Do not ever tell a seeker that they or someone in their life is going to die. You are not God, you do not know the timing of anyone's death.

NEGATIVITY

A reading can have some negativity from the cards but have enough positive cards to balance the reading out. Occasionally, you will encounter a reading that is so negative it is hard to find anything positive to give the seeker.

Be gentle. The seeker needs to hear this negative story. It has come because of a need, but find words that give the story in a considered way. Always remind the seeker that their actions will change much. A seemingly simple step may create an entirely different layout.

3
TAROT SPREADS

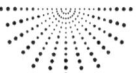

As with decks, there are a multitude of Tarot spreads available to you. As our world changes, Tarot readers add more interesting spreads to suit our times and psychological knowledge. Creative and knowledgeable readers develop spreads that help readers connect to the current language and culture of today.

For a beginning reader start simple. Use the spreads described in this book. This will allow you to easily build your knowledge of the cards, and also of placement of the cards in the spreads. Knowing which placement is what is important so you don't wrongly interpret the layout. For example, say that a card placed in a present spot is a future card.

Once you have grasped the basic spreads - Three-Card, Celtic Cross and Horoscope spread, you can work with other spreads and find those that work for you. A good knowledge of a variety of spreads will allow you to select more precisely what will work for specific readings and questions.

Three-Card Spread

The Three Card Spread is great for a quick and simple consultation. It can be used first thing in the morning before you start your day, or when you require a general insight into a situation. This spread is recommended to be used often when you are first learning the Tarot as it is simple and will give you the experience of interpreting the cards.

- **Card #2** for the Present, is the first card drawn. The card is illustrating the current problem. Sometimes the problem stems from Card #1. Card #2 can also show any obstacles that may be in the way
- **Card #1** is the Past, placed to the left of Card #2. This card is showing the current situation and the influences that put the seeker there – possibly a person, a job or relationship
- **Card #3** is drawn and placed to the right of Card #2. Card 3 gives the seeker advice on how to overcome the issue. Look for options and guidance in this card
- A variation is Card #2 representing the seeker's Mind, Card #1, the seeker's Body and Card #3 the seeker's Spirit

Remember that when you use this spread for a general reading you may not have an issue, or at least one that you are aware of yet. In a question asking, "How will my day be?", the Past card would show you yesterday's influences, the Present card, what is in place today and what you should consider as you go through your day, while the Future card gives the outcome of the day.

As in all Tarot spreads, the card's position in the layout and the cards surrounding it, influence how the card is currently 'speaking'. In multi card layouts, all cards need to be considered. Don't interpret the past, present and future cards in isolation. Create a story. How did the past card influence today and the future? What will today's card bring to the future?

Celtic Cross Spread

The Celtic Cross is the traditional spread that you may have encountered or seen. While it gives an in-depth reading, it may be a difficult spread to interpret. Take your time to learn and spend time on the interconnections between the cards. You can read the individual cards with their meaning as it pertains to their placement in the cross, but the true depth comes from seeing the inter-relationships and the story that is portrayed by viewing all the cards together. This spread has layers, upon layers. It tells a story and learning to read and tell the story is the hard work.

There are different orders of layout of the cards in the Celtic Cross spread. The order of cards 3, 4, 5, & 6 may vary depending on the reader's preference. (Eden Gray vs Waite). If you use a signifier, it is placed first and the first card covers it.

It is possible to use just the Major Arcana in this layout. If you are learning, this may be a good way for you to concentrate on the Major Arcana cards and their interactions. The Celtic Cross is a good spread to use regularly as you are learning the Tarot. It will hone not just your individual card knowledge, but also the interactions between the cards. Consider how the foundation card helped create the past. Look at how the immediate outcome will influence the longer term outcome. The foundation card influences what goal the seeker is moving towards.

The first step is to learn the individual placements:

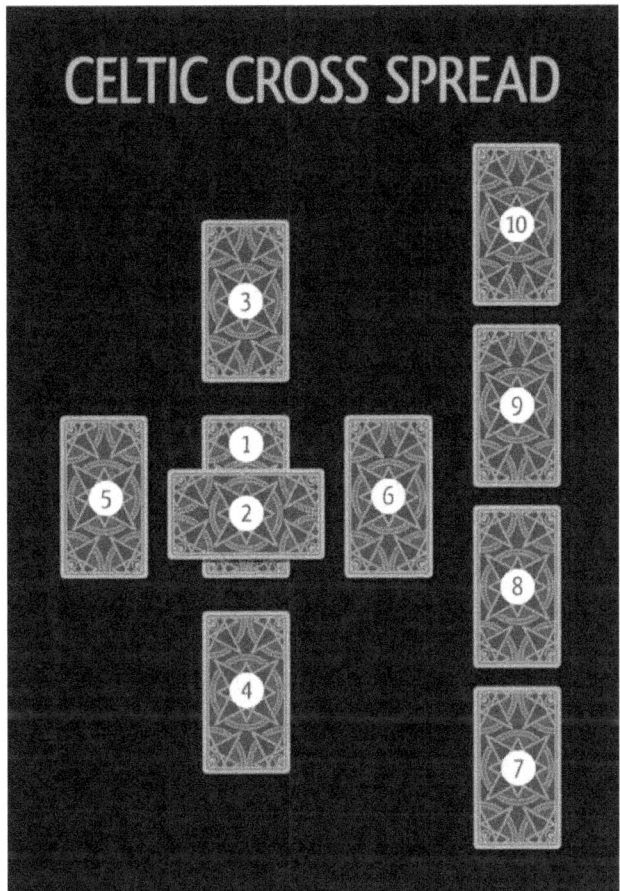

- **Card 1: The Current State:** What is currently happening to the seeker. The heart of the matter
- **Card 2: The Problem/ Forces that Oppose the Seeker:** The obstacle or issue that is facing the seeker. This usually represents the question that seeker wants answered. This card is also known as the Crossing card
- **Card 3: Above/Goals/Aspirations:** The seekers goal, what they wish for in the situation
- **Card 4: The Foundation / Subconscious:** The unconscious of the seeker including hidden feelings and emotions attached

to the situation. What the issue is building on or the root of the problem
- **Card 5: The Immediate Past:** This reflects events and people that have contributed to the current challenge. These events have passed out of the seeker's life or are in the process of passing out
- **Card 6: The Immediate Future:** What may happen in the next few days or weeks. This is not the final conclusion of the issue. It does not predict the future but gives possibilities based on your reactions and where the cards lay at the moment. Your thoughts, unconscious or conscious, and your actions can change this card
- **Card 7: Advice:** What the seeker can do to deal with the issue
- **Card 8: External Influences:** Shows the people (family, friends, co-workers etc.) and energy that are influencing the situation. These are not in the seeker's control. It also shows how others around you are viewing the situation
- **Card 9: Hopes and Fears:** Hopes and fears of the seeker. Look for internal conflicts that the seeker may be experiencing. This card often expresses the seeker's values
- **Card 10: Outcome:** The resolution of the issue or if no resolution, where the situation will land

The second step in reading the Celtic Cross spread is to look at the combinations and pull the story from it.

- Examine the interplay between the Above and Subconscious cards. Is there conflict between the two or are they aligned?
- Consider the relations between the Above, Subconscious, and Outcome cards. Are they generally compatible, moving towards the same goals or is there conflict?
- How is the immediate Future contributing to the Outcome? Does it conflict with any of the other cards?
- Reflect on how the seeker's Hopes and Fears are influencing the Future and Outcome cards

- Compare the Advice card with the other cards. If the seeker followed the advice, what might change in the card layout?

The Horoscope Spread

The Horoscope spread is a powerful spread to dig deep into certain areas of seeker's life, goals and past. A good time to use this spread is at the beginning of a year – either the New Year or on a seeker's birthday. It can be done monthly or every few months to gain updates and further insight.

The Horoscope spread is a Zodiac chart, with each card representing an astrological house, or area of life. It looks like a clock and the cards are layout based on a circular analogue clock.

Each card in this layout represents one of the 12 astrological houses. After shuffling the cards, choose the 1st card and place it at 9'o'clock (Left middle). Place the next card below it and continue to draw cards and place them according to a clock time, moving anticlockwise.

- **House: Self/ Identity.** Placed at 9 o'clock. Shows the seekers personality, physicality, and psychology. This can be the self the seeker is projecting to others. *Associations:* Fire, Wands, Aries, Mars
- **House: Money/Wealth.** Placed at 8 o'clock. Indicates the seeker's worth, money, and possessions. Can show the seeker's earning power. *Associations:* Earth, Pentacles, Taurus, Venus
- **House: Mental Activity/Communication**. Placed at 7 o'clock. What you know and think, your community and family. *Associations:* Air, Swords, Gemini, Mercury
- **House: Emotions/ Home/Family.** Placed at 6 o'clock. Reflects the seeker's attachments, roots, home, and history. *Associations:* Water, Cups, Cancer, the Moon
- **House: Creativity & Children.** Placed at 5 o'clock. Describes the seeker's artistic talent. Giving birth. Play and romance. *Associations:* Fire, Wands, Leo, the Sun
- **House: Work/Service**. Placed at 4 o'clock. The day-to-day life of the seeker, their responsibilities, and job. *Associations:* Earth, Pentacles, Virgo, Mercury
- **House: Partnerships.** Placed at 3 o'clock. This card deals with committed romantic or business partnerships. Where these relationships will move over the coming times. *Associations:* Air, Swords, Libra, Venus
- **House: External Influences**. Placed at 2 o'clock. Death, taxes, and shared resources. Other people who can influence or interfere in the seeker's life. *Associations:* Water, Cups, Scorpio, Pluto
- **House: Learning/Changing.** Placed at 1 o'clock. Where the seeker can expand. Education, courses, changing beliefs,

religion and philosophy. Travel experiences. *Associations:* Fire, Wands, Sagittarius, Jupiter
- **House: Career.** Placed at 12 o'clock. Career is different from a job. A job might be used to pay for a course or to pass time. A career is a chosen path using skills, innate or learned. Can cover the seeker's reputation as it relates to a career. *Associations:* Earth, Pentacles, Capricorn, Saturn
- **House: Goals/Dreams**. Placed at 11 o'clock. The seeker's desires and what they are striving towards. *Associations:* Air, Swords, Aquarius, Uranus
- **House: Spirituality.** Placed at 10 o'clock. Karmic lessons, spiritual beliefs, subconscious desires. *Associations:* Water, Cups, Pisces

PART II
THE MAJOR ARCANA

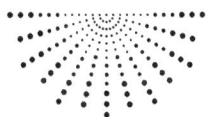

There are 21 numbered Major Arcana cards plus 1 unnumbered card, The Fool (0) for a total of 22 cards. Also known as the Trumps, each Major Arcana card represents a specific Jungian archetypal individual. The Major Arcana cards are richly illustrated, displaying the symbolism related to the card.

There are 12 Jungian archetypes:

- Hero
- Sovereign
- Magician
- Sage
- Creator
- Jester
- Innocent
- Explorer
- Rebel
- Lover
- Citizen
- Caregiver

Some of the archetypes in the Tarot are obvious (Magician), others take deeper knowledge to relate the car to the archetype.

The Major Arcana Tarot cards represent the life lessons influencing your life. The card meanings are complex and require deep thought to interpret. The cards access the unconsciousness of the seeker and are firmly rooted in an archetypal context. Major Arcana cards deal with the bigger part of life and give perspective and guidance.

When several Major Arcana cards are in a Tarot spread, it indicates that the reading has important lessons for the seeker. The seeker can expect major impacts on their life. The cards are telling the seeker to pay attention. The reader should apply their knowledge and create a story from the cards meaning and their position, carefully considering the inter-relationships between the cards.

A single Major Arcana card in a reading requires attention as well and should be considered carefully in perspective with the other cards. Reflect on the card's theme and archetype.

As stated in the introduction, the Major Arcana tells a story, using The Fool as the main character. The Fool moves takes a journey, encountering each of the cards and their lessons on the way, reaching completion at the World card. Following The Fool's journey can help the new reader in learning the meanings and understanding the Tarot process.

1
THE FOOL

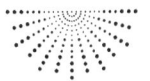

Card 0, The Fool, is a powerful card in the Tarot deck. Court de Gebelin places The Fool as the zero or negative card[1] as it simultaneously represents new beginnings and endings. The Fool speaks of a journey, the beginning of a life path that will give you direction and focus. New births are not without hazards, and The Fool is there to remind you to calculate the risk factors before leaping into the unknown.

When we look at The Fool, he seems to almost dance with delight. We are reminded to be courageous and take risks without unnecessarily putting yourself at harm. For without those risks. you will not learn; you will miss many adventures and joys. You will remain stuck in a world without change or newness. The Fool almost walks on air, so eager is he to proceed on his life path. He is youthful, full of innocence and naivety.

The Fool card depicts a young person (neither male nor female nor trans), dressed as a court jester, walking joyfully in the world. Taking the first steps away from home, he is exuberant, excited, and full of joy. A white sun blazes in the sky, representing power. He carries nothing with him except a small sack attached to the wand in his right hand. In The Fool's left hand, he holds a white rose, indicating innocence and growth. Gazing up to the sky and the larger world, he seems to be ignoring the possible dangers on his path. If The Fool doesn't take care, he will soon encounter the first of these dangers. One more step, and he will fall over the cliff that he is nearing. He seems unconcerned. Is he naive or merely unaware? The Fool leads a simple, minimalist life with no worries and is not troubled by future concerns. To him, change is exciting.

The small dog at his heel barks a warning, trying to make the youth aware of the edge of the cliff. There are lessons to learn, and if The Fool is careful, it won't be disastrous. As long he is aware, he will probably do no more than skin his knees and elbows as he runs into obstacles and dangers.

At the same time, this little dog encourages The Fool in his adventures, pushing him to the cliff edge. If The Fool does not pay attention, he may never see all the adventures that he is daydreaming about, for hard-learned lessons on the way could sideline him. The mountains behind The Fool represent the challenges the Fool will encounter out in the world. But The Fool is ignoring them. He is focused on his present. He is naïve, but that naivety allows him to be open to the magic of life. Worrying about the future and what lies ahead restricts your vision, causing you to stumble in the here and now. If you look too far forward, you may not see what is right in front of you.

The dog represents The Fool's intuition, which guides him as he walks along. The Fool doesn't need weapons to defend himself; he doesn't need to cower in a cave afraid of what might happen. He only needs to pay attention to his intuition and allow his gut to guide him on the correct path.

With his youthfulness and playful air, The Fool represents the bountiful potential of spring. Enhancing this vision is The Fool's card number of 0, representing infinite potential. He is at the beginning, carrying no baggage or emotional scars. The Fool is seeking adventures on his journey, for these adventures will create growth and maturity. No matter where we are in life, The Fool allows us to begin again and make a fresh start. The Fool is a classic archetype, one that appears in many cultures: a *trickster*, the *clever fox*, *coyote*.

The Fool often shows up in a reading when you're moving from one stage in life to the next. This could include leaving high school, graduating from college, marriage, pregnancy, changing careers, moving to a new home, or retiring. The Fool asks you for faith; to leap ahead and go for it. Research the impacts but don't spend too much time investigating and worrying about outcomes. When you don't grab an opportunity, you may see it slip away. The Fool does not hesitate. Follow your heart, and all will work out. Remember that you have skills and are capable; you are not venturing out unaided. When your life is changing, rely on your knowledge. Your unconscious will guide you into the future.

When the Fool appears in a card layout, it can mean new beginnings are coming into your life. These new beginnings are filled with an optimistic outlook and joy. Free from the chains of your past experiences, your journey is open to all possibilities such as travel, a new career, starting a family, a new exercise regime, or a new relationship. Start each day with curiosity to see what adventures await you. Let lightness fill your soul and believe that anything can and will happen. It may take practice and determination, but you will be rewarded.

That said, The Fool can cause issues. If you show a lack of discipline or an inability to control yourself, the Fool may negatively influence your life. The Fool doesn't give you permission to ignore your responsibilities or be inconsiderate of others. He doesn't ask you to ignore significant risks but rather to judge the possible impacts of any choice.

The Fool also doesn't guarantee the outcome. Outcomes depend on your abilities to exercise judgement and to use your knowledge wisely. Remember, the Fool is 0. As he is nothing, the 0 card, the way is wide open, a new beginning stretches before us. He is the start of bringing something into reality, and you have many more steps to go. His presence is a good omen for your journey, for he represents the unlimited potential of your path. Embrace your unique challenges and trust that you will learn the skills you require for this new adventure. Be playful, energetic, and flexible. Let go of any expectations and be open to the newness. Above all, trust your intuition.

The Fool is known by different names including:

- Le Mat (madman)
- Il Matto (the beggar)
- Joker
- The Excuse
- Maut (Egyptian Vulture Goddess)
- Dalua (great fool of the Celts)
- Percival (Knight of the round table)
- The Jester
- Mate
- Unwise Man

NUMBER 0 SYMBOLISM

The Fool's card number is 0. Zero contains everything and nothing. According to Crowley in the Book of Thoth, 'it represents the Negative above the Tree of Life, the source of all things."[2] Zero contains an unlimited potential, and because it is numbered zero, The Fool can be placed either at the beginning or the end of the Major Arcana.

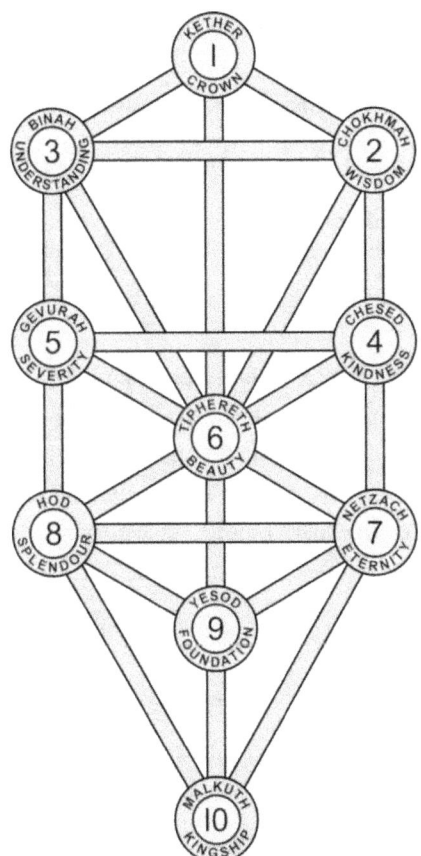

The Major Arcana is often considered The Fool's journey through life.

On the Tree of Life, The Fool's path is Aleph, from Kether to Chokhmah. Aleph is Hebrew for the letter A and represents indefinite possibilities. Kether is the force of spirit, the youthful energy that moves you forward. At the same time, Chokhmah brings The Fool to his foundations, the beginnings of his journey. This is the nameless path of zero leading from the Crown to the Wisdom. So too, The Fool has unlimited potential and therefore needs no number.

Following this path opens you up to new ways of thinking, bringing forth your creativity and allowing you to change. You are The Fool who embraces the challenges of life. While on this path, be fearless, forget worry, and relax because ultimately, it all ends in nothingness. When you travel this path, you are on a journey of freedom, opening yourself to opportunities and creativity. You become the inventor of your life. You are not just following mindlessly along. This is the path of uniqueness, of the inventor, the quirky. The Fool belongs on this path.

On the flip side of this path are the challenges of being The Fool. The Fool can be unpredictable and unstable. While on this path, you risk becoming inconsistent and irresponsible. As always, it is about balance.

Notice that The Fool's cloak is covered with 10 yellow circles. These circles represent emanations of the Kabbalah. In the Kabbalah, The Fool is associated with Aleph, a starting point with the element of air. Aleph, as The Fool, represents the silence before creation. The Fool is the beginning, and the last, balancing opposites; male and female, mother and father, good/evil.

CHAKRA

The Crown chakra is the chakra of Divine Oneness and symbolized by violet or white thousand-petalled lotus. This chakra represents pure consciousness and bliss. It is an energy center that functions at its best when you let go of your ego's need to be in charge.

Known as Sahasrara in Sanskrit, the Crown chakra is the seventh chakra. Located on the crown of the head, and associated with spirituality, the Crown chakra allows people to move from materialism to the wholeness of spirituality. Opening the crown chakra brings insight and confidence to your life.

While the Root chakra grounds us to the Earth, the Crown chakra's energy joins us to the universal whole and the creation of newness. With this chakra, you experience oneness and a feeling that everything is connected at the source. Your crown chakra emanates a peaceful and calm feeling.

Starting at 0, The Fool shows the joy and feeling of spring within this chakra. Neither cynicism nor encountered challenges have developed – the kind that leaves you with baggage and closed to opportunities, love, or the simple pleasures of life. Instead, you are open and appreciate the vitality around you, full of gratitude for the moments.

CORRESPONDENCE

- **Astrology:** Aries, ruling planet is Uranus
- **Rune:** Jera: good harvest. Your efforts are realized, peace and happiness.
- **I Ching:** Hexagram 25 (Innocence): The man is innocent and true. Stick to your true nature and values and you will succeed
- **Symbol:** White rose
- **Animal:** Dog
- **Element:** Air

READING CARD PLACEMENT

The Fool is telling you to let go of expectations and trust your intuition. The position of The Fool in your spread reveals the areas of your life that may be changing or have changed. The Fool can indicate essential decisions are about to be made (or have been made). You are being offered a choice. These decisions could involve risks, going your own path, or allow for more creativity in your life. This choice will have a large impact on your life, for a long time, so take the time to understand. Be optimistic to gain the most of The Fool's journey. He gives hope. The Fool symbolizes your complete surrender to the divine source.

Past

Your intuition and the risks you took have brought you to where you currently abide. The newness generated opportunities and options for you. You used your creativity and wisdom to create solutions in all aspects of your life. You didn't resist the change. Instead, you took hold and allowed The Fool to guide you. Take a chance.

Present

You have entered a new phase in your life. The impact may not yet be shown, but it will become evident to you. Assess the risks, use your intuition, and have confidence. In the present position, The Fool signifies that you are gaining independence and there may be adventures shortly coming your way. The Fool is a potent card. Use your intuition to remove obstacles and embrace your new-found life.

Future

Opportunities and change are on the horizon. Listen with your heart and allow your intuition to guide you to a new direction or path. Grab opportunities; don't hesitate and let them disappear. Create newness and be independent. Embrace your freedom. Be willing to change and be open to what the universe is handing you. You can find the changes anywhere: in love, your family, your career, your values. Maybe you'll move or change your life in a significant manner. Wherever this newness appears, use your creativity to develop it to its fullness.

YES / NO KEY INTERPRETATION

The answer to your question is yes. Remember to be open as you explore the options. Don't jump without looking around but don't let yourself be caught up in worry. Use your intuition to guide you forward. Be creative in the solution.

KEYWORDS

Freedom, potential, fresh starts, uniqueness, beginnings, freedom, independence, generation of ideas, innocence, naiveté, creativity.

2
THE MAGICIAN

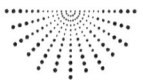

The Magician entices. Wearing magician robes, his appearance shows everything; confidence, knowledge, spells, and his well-known trickery. Instinctively you want what he has but are also slightly afraid of him, of what cards he might pull from behind his back. Or how he might reveal secrets that you have hidden away. The Magician, however, is a very positive card, bringing the power of his mastery and the universe to you. This is your time to use these powers to control your mind, create your life and complete your goals.

The Magician card is the first numbered card in the Tarot Deck. It is 1, the number of new opportunities. He is your bridge between the spirit world and the physical world. The Magician is correlated with the High Priestess and considered a messenger of God. With his right hand reaching the spirits in the sky, his left-hand points to the earth, grounding himself to earthly consciousness while bringing the spiritual to the earth. "As above, so below, as within, so without, as the universe, so the soul…" Hermes Trismegistus. [1]

Above his head, the infinity sign hangs, symbolizing eternal life and spiritual attainment. In front of the table, the roses and lilies illustrate the creativity and fertility he conveys to you, manifested when the universe brings your goals into fruition. Circling The Magician's waist is a snake eating his tail, another symbol of eternal life and unlimited potential. It also illustrates The Magician's connection to the unconscious.

The table in front of him signifies reality, the foundations of life. On The Magician's table are four symbolic items that represent the four Tarot decks:

- a wand (fire/physical action)
- a cup (water/emotions)
- a sword (air/mental processes)
- a pentacle (earth/money/material items)

The Magician has mastered all aspects of The Tarot, displaying his skill and power. He can easily bring forth dreams and desires. He is often unexpected and therefore gains his reputation as the trickster. He is a strong individual with a solid spiritual center.

In front of the table are rows of roses. Red roses are a sign of goddesses and the feminine. The Magician has carefully balanced his internal energies.

An intelligent and highly disciplined man, The Magician is both creative and a great communicator. The opposite of the High Priestess card his presence in a layout indicates you are moving from analysis to action by using your talents. The Magician tells you to use discipline and think through your actions. Be determined to succeed. Use your intelligence and creativity to walk your daily path and apply self-control in using your spirituality and emotions. Channel the power to apply yourself. Ensure you bring spirit into your process, allowing your spiritual self to surface as you work away in the material world.

The Magician tells you that success is possible. It is time for action; to begin projects. If you hold back and deny yourself, you may lose the opportunity to transform your life. Make changes, pursue goals. You can change your life, be it a career, relationships, family, or developing a creative venture. Remember that baby steps take us where we need to go. Create your goals and move forward on the path to completion. "Whatever you can do or dream you can, begin it. Boldness has genius, power, and magic in it" Johann Wolfgang von Goethe.

The Magician can also represent deception. He is known as the Trickster, after all. Watch for any deceit or negativity as you explore your options and move forward. Don't let yourself be diverted from your path or stop yourself from doing what you need to do. If you stop, you will end up with nothing.

On the flip side, The Magician can cause you to be over-confident. Always research your options and ensure they are grounded in reality. Take the time to think and explore without doing a full stop. And know that ultimately, The Magician is on your side.

The Magician is known by other names including:

- Sage
- Wizard
- Merlin
- Le Batelent
- Le Bateleur (Bearer of the Baton)
- Teacher
- The Juggler
- Hermes

NUMBER 1 SYMBOLISM

In the tarot card deck, The Magician is the first numbered card of the Major Arcana associated with the number 1 and the first letter of the Hebrew alphabet 'Beth', which means house. The number 1 represents individuality, creativity, originality, power, knowledge, and birth. It stands for unity and the beginning of all. This beginning is continued in the meaning of the cards that follow. Being the first official card in the Major Arcana, confirms The Magician's connection to the Divine. Number 1 is also is associated with the sun. In Christianity, the number 1 is a symbol of the unity between God and Jesus and is significant as the Bible indicates there is only 1 God.

The number 1 begins all our opportunities. This number shows us our current life and gives you the understanding that you have the power to make changes and produce what you yearn for in this life. The number 1 tells you to create your own way and not wait for others to produce it for you. Like The Magician, the number 1 has achieved goals and is always moving forward, not content to sit idle.

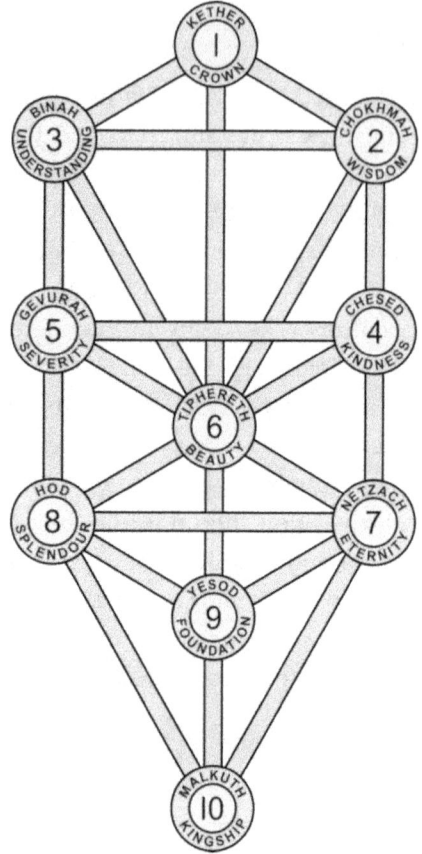

On the Tree of Life, The Magician is linked to path 2, which is found between Kether (Spirit or Crown) and Binah (Divine Mother). This path carries the will of God. We see the beginning of duality, the creator and created. Considered the spiritual path, it consists of the Self, the path to God, and God himself. When walking this road, the goal is to blend the three into one, for that is the way to genuine knowledge. You need to regularly check to ensure that you are not missing one of these aspects as you walk forward to your goals.

The number 1 is only divisible by itself, remaining independent from other numbers. It is the number of creation, from which all other numbers emerge. While independent, 1 is a leader, having the strength and determination to move others to a goal. This leader is able to separate right from wrong and navigate The Magician's path through any deception or trickery.

CHAKRA

The magician is related to the fifth chakra, the Throat chakra. The Throat chakra provides emotional strength and determination to The Magician, so you can do your work. The Throat chakra gives you the sound and vibration of energy in our body. This chakra enhances communication and allows you to express yourself truthfully. It moves energy between your head and your body.

The Throat chakra is called Vishuddha (or Pure) and is located in the center of the neck on the throat. Its symbol has sixteen petals of a smoky-purple color, representing the Throat chakra's sixteen energies. This chakra allows you to tell the world about yourself, your values, goals, and purpose. The Throat chakra helps us express and project our dreams and visions into the world.

This chakra, like The Magician, is your connection to the spirit world and our intuitive abilities. The two help you create and move your dreams into reality. If your Throat Chakra is blocked, your ability to realize your purpose in life will be hampered. Use The Magician's skills to open your Throat chakra, allowing your intuition to come to the forefront once again.

CORRESPONDENCE

- **Astrology:** Aries: Ruled by the planets Mercury and the Sun
- **Rune:** Mannaz: mankind
- **I Ching:** Hexagram 29 (Danger): This hexagram represents your soul. Be sincere and you will have success
- **Symbol:** Lily: symbol of truth and humility
- **Animal:** Fox
- **Element**: Earth

READING CARD PLACEMENT

The appearance of The Magician in a reading is a powerful omen. When The Magician hands you skills, your life can change significantly. He doesn't just bring newness to you; you must work hard and use your potential to create the magic in your life. The Magician delivers the tools you require to manifest your dreams. He brings the spiritual (fire), physical (earth), mental (air), and emotional (water) resources that you require to move your goals from fantasy to reality. When the Magician appears in a reading, he is telling you to move forward. Take action.

To create, you need both a vision and goals. Check your intuition and values to ensure your goals align and will bring you a healthy future. The Magician brings potential; it is up to you to take action and bring that potential to life.

Past

You used your creativity and grabbed onto an opportunity with success in the past. Continue to move forward. Don't let your gains slip away with inaction. The Magician will continue to provide you with power.

Present

The Magician is guiding you and giving you the potential to realize your dreams. This is the time to use your power. You might be seeking a new job, opening a business or falling in love. Whatever the goal or vision, The Magician is giving you the signal to take action. Don't hold back, or opportunities will slip through your fingers. Use The Magician's power and your skills to fulfill your dreams and expand your creativity.

Future

The future brings creativity and opportunity. Use your skill to harness the power of The Magician. Success is available to you, with new beginnings. Prepare yourself, so you are ready when it appears. Get started on your goals now, so the power of The Magician is used to its full force. Be confident.

YES / NO KEY INTERPRETATION

The answer to your question is yes. The Magician is there for you. Take action. Manifest your destiny.

KEYWORDS

Will power, manifestation, action, power, confidence, success.

3

THE HIGH PRIESTESS

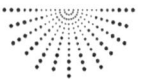

The High Priestess sits in front of a temple veil which is embroidered with pomegranates, representing the conscious and subconscious areas of our thoughts. Pomegranates are a symbol of abundance, fertility, and femininity. The moon at The High Priestess's feet indicates her grounding in intuition and psychic ability. She holds the Torah scrolls.

On either side of the High Priestess are the pillars that guard the entrance to the temple. The left pillar is black with the letter B for Boaz (strength), while the right pillar is white with the letter J for Jachin (establishment). Black and white personify the dual nature of life: masculine and feminine, darkness and light, good and evil, positive and negative.

The High Priestess serves as a mediator between the two sides. Think of her as the way through, showing you the path between the two pillars. Neither pillar is good or bad; they both contain knowledge that will aid you on your path. The crown the High Priestess wears is the crown of Isis. She is a ruler, a queen, wearing a solar cross around her neck, illustrating her connection and grounding to the earth. The crescent moon at her feet symbolizes her association with the gods and her ability to use intuition and your own subconscious mind to guide you.

The High Priestess holds a scroll printed with the letters TORA. The scroll contains sacred knowledge, revealed to you over time as you learn and gain wisdom. The High Priestess reminds you to open your mind and spirit, for that is how real insight is gained. She rules the hidden and knows your secrets. When you use your intuition to understand a situation, the High Priestess is the one who reveals the truth.

The High Priestess lets you know that instinct is needed right now, not reason or logic. Trust your heart and subconscious. Look for signs and omens to guide you. There are times in life when only your intuition or your gut can honestly counsel and assist you with a situation. When you use your intuition, The High Priestess will warn you of hidden influences.

The High Priestess is also called:

- Isis
- Joan
- The Popess

NUMBER 2 SYMBOLISM

The second numbered card in the deck, the High Priestess, teaches you how to develop the skills of The Magician. As you use your instinct to find the right path for you, the number 2, as a symbol of gestation, eventually leads to development and forward movement. Two is a feminine number, as women gestate babies, so 2 gestates ideas.

The number 2 also stands for trust. Trust that while you are in this gestation period, your inspiration will guide you, and all is unfolding as it is meant to be. Have faith that you will find what you are seeking.

The High Priestess is associated with the 2nd Path on the Tree of Life (Chokmah), which connects Kether (Crown) and Tiferet (Beauty). This path is often called 'Unifying Intelligence' as it unites Kether, Chokmah, and Binah. The 2nd Path deals with transformation and asks you to clear out the old to make room for the new. It clears out the chaos, allowing you to believe in your intuition and gain wisdom.

THE HIGH PRIESTESS | 47

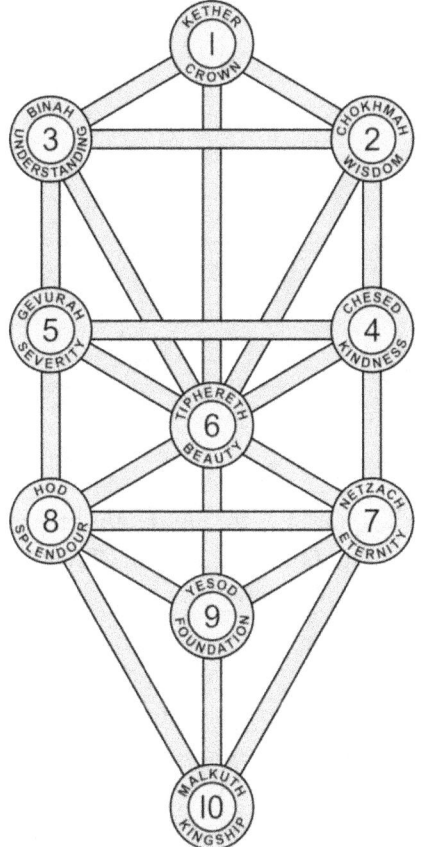

Like the pillars on the High Priestess card, Chokmah balances good and evil and all opposites in life. Creativity runs between 2 opposing factions, and the 2nd path aids you in finding the perfect symmetry.

Number 2 is also about opposites, for 2 cannot stand alone. It is about duality and, like Chokmah, creating unity. It's about finding the in-between, the place that allows you to hold yourself with 2 pluralities and connect with both.

The number 2 tells you to be gentle with yourself and others. Develop the kind of deep understanding that allows you to see below the surface, becoming resourceful and a survivor. Use the High Priestess's gifts to show you the way. Learn how the number 2 bends with the wind and how to carry weight without destroying you.

The corresponding planet of this card is the Moon. The Moon suggests that this Tarot card contains female energy.

CHAKRA

The chakra corresponding to the High Priestess is the second chakra, the Sacral chakra. Located 2 inches below the navel and vibrant orange in color, it affects the reproductive system, sexual organs, and the lumbar plexus.

Like the High Priestess, this chakra is the center of your creativity, connecting you with your desires and ambitions. The Sacral chakra looks for pleasure, the fun things in life. In Sanskrit, it is called Svadhishthana (abode, your home). The High Priestess rules your unconscious and connects to the Sacral chakra to expose your yearnings, those that have meaning, value, and depth for you. She seeks to awaken you and show you everything that is hidden away in your unconscious. The 2nd chakra helps her with this goal.

The Sacral chakra connects you to spirit. As it brings your unconscious dreams into the light, it opens your ability to appreciate life and be joyful. You learn to enjoy life to its fullest. With this chakra, you can use the power of the High Priestess to create a new life. The High Priestess encourages you to be open and live in the moment. If this chakra is closed, the High Priestess can't speak to you and reveal her knowledge. When the 2nd chakra is open, you feel the change and transformation occurring, and you welcome it.

This chakra is associated with your emotions and feelings. It contributes to how you feel and express yourself. The sacral chakra rules our fantasies, those dreams that the High Priestess wants to bring into the light so you can evaluate them and consider your options. If something is hidden, your unconscious can cause you to do inappropriate things. Or appropriate but only when brought forth at the right time. When you examine these visions, you will gain understanding as to how they will impact your life. You will have the knowledge to know if and when you should act on them. You become the driver of your own bus, not just the passenger sliding through life.

CORRESPONDENCES

- **Astrology:** Pisces: watery depths where things are
- hidden. Element is water
- **Rune:** Pethro: secrets and inner knowledge
- **I Ching:** Hexagram 61 Zhong Fu (Inner Truth): letting your unconscious come to the surface. Be open to the truth. It is a sign of good fortune3..
- **Symbol:** The Moon: hidden secrets
- **Animal:** Wolf
- **Element:** Water

READING CARD PLACEMENT

The High Priestess's appearance in a layout informs you that it is time to listen to your intuition and bring your unconscious to light. This is not a time for intellectualizing or justifying your actions. The answer to your questions is hidden in your own depths. This card reminds you to be open, let your unconscious desires come forth. She brings a feminine side to the issue before you. She is a successful woman in a male dominated world.

Past

The High Priestess gave you knowledge: knowledge that came from the depths, knowledge that you hid from yourself. If you used this knowledge wisely and trusted your instincts, you are on the path to developing your dreams. If you ignored this knowledge, you might experience negative impacts in the present.

Present

Your intuition is giving you information. Your unconscious mind is coming into the light, and you must listen to it. Any issues or concerns can be resolved using this knowledge. If you use logic and rational thinking to develop your goals and dreams, you may miss a valuable experience that could change the outcome. Trust yourself, trust your inner voice.

Future

A time is coming where you will need to rely on your intuition, not your thinking or analytical skills. To prepare for this, start listening now and let it guide you. Your unconscious knows you better than you think. There may be a woman arriving who can assist you in accessing your hidden knowledge.

YES / NO KEY INTERPRETATION

The answer to your question is unclear. The High Priestess is full of mystery and wisdom. Things are yet to be uncovered. Listen to your intuition to find the answer.

KEYWORDS

Intuition, knowledge, the subconscious mind, bringing things into the light.

4

THE EMPRESS

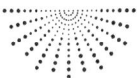

Regardless of the deck, the image of The Empress is always full and fertile. She isn't skinny or drawn. The Empress portrays a sense of fruitfulness and creativity. The Empress brings to mind Carl Jung's archetypes in his theory of the human psyche. Archetypes are the universal depths that connect with others at the same deep unconscious level – the collective unconscious. When we examine the Empress card, our emotions awake, and our unconscious understands who she is and what she represents to us.

As an archetype of feminine power, the Empress brings much to our understanding of what it means to be a woman. Mysterious and creative, The Empress is also sexual and fertile. She challenges all genders to acknowledge female power. As a spiritual power, The Empress helps you define your future, giving you dreams and desires to improve your life. She wants you to add creativity to your life, leading you to understand that there is more, a significant place for you. She urges you to expand your life, your work, your productivity, and become fertile with imagination.

The main image on this card is the Empress herself. Often shown as pregnant, she is a woman who exudes fertility while remaining peaceful and content. The crown of stars The Empress wears symbolizes her mysticism, while her robe, decorated with pomegranates, is symbolic of fertility. Sitting on a throne with a red cushion, stitched with the sign of Venus, The Empress holds an in orb her hand, gifting her with the power of rule, while a shield leans against her chair. The shield displays the universal symbol for woman. She is a beautiful, victorious and passionate woman.

In the background is a forest, with a stream. Water expresses your emotions, bringing hidden feelings to the surface. The stream indicates the Empress's ability to connect not only with her own feelings, but also with the earth. Nature rejuvenates us all, and here the Empress gathers strength from the energy of nature. There is wheat dancing in the air; this is fertile ground supplying you with food and other gifts.

The Empress brings you the power and spiritual wisdom to be free to improve your life beyond your own expectations. Like a bird, your spirit can fly high, full of energy, and confidence. Representing Mother

Earth, The Empress expresses herself through her feminine, fertile, and abundant nature. When channeling the Empress in you, you are creative, give birth, and grow your garden. She provides you with harmony, fertility, and beauty. The Empress helps you imagine ideas and nurture them into existence. In many decks, she is pregnant, bringing forth life, both literally and figuratively. Both Demeter, the Roman goddess of agriculture, and Freyja, the Norse god of fertility, are images of the Empress.

The Empress also brings you romance. For without that flash of attraction, life cannot be created. Freud claimed that creativity comes from sexual attraction to the opposite sex, which the Empress generates for us. The Empress causes change and renewal, forcing you to move into the future. The Empress asks you to be open to change. Forget your past. Let her guide you with all her passion. Use your intuition, trust your gut, your heart, and your unconscious.

If you deny this passion or block your intuition, you may be put on the wrong journey. You may take jobs, loves, or opportunities that you should have let pass by. Or you may ignore paths that you should have jumped onto - ones that would have led you to triumph. Use your self-control and patience. She is not asking you to stop or to wait for a long time or be over cautious. She is only asking that you listen for what is real for you, for what will work with your values and life over the long run.

Like all Tarot cards, The Empress card must always be evaluated with the surrounding cards. This will help you understand exactly what she is saying, what area of your life she is focusing on, and what time frame. The Empress is a positive card to receive. She aids you in whatever quest you are on. Even if she warns you, it is with optimism and guidance that allows you to be successful. The Empress seeks balance in all.

The Empress holds the key to save both those close to her and Mother Earth. She expresses unconditional love to all. Seeing what needs to be done to help others along their path, The Empress uses her skills wisely to assist all. She doesn't force you but asks that you stop and listen. Ponder her gifts to you.

The Empress is sometimes called:

- Daleth
- Freyr
- Demeter
- Venus
- Aphrodite
- Goddess of Love

NUMBER 3 SYMBOLISM

The Empress card is numbered 3 in the Rider Waite Tarot decks. Number 3 is a number of creativity. Like a deep river, she flows forward into the future

past rocks, dams, and rapids. Her river represents life itself, and in the Kabbalah, the Tree of Life represent those associations. On the Tree of Life, the Empress sits between Chokmah and Binah (emanation), which like the number 3 of The Empress card, indicates understanding and unity.

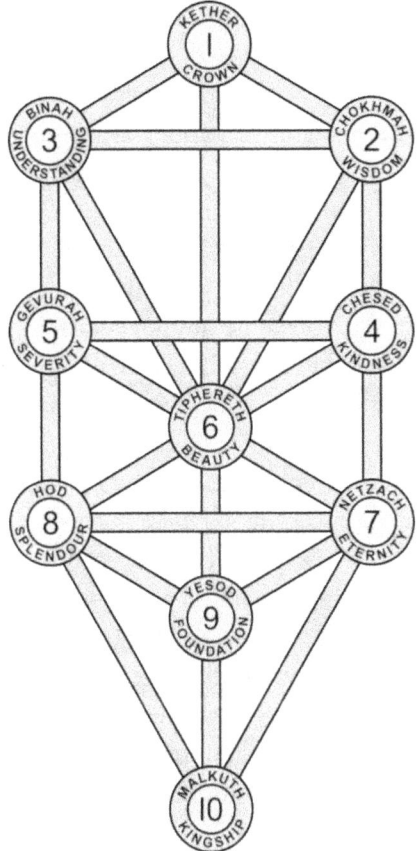

In old religions, you encounter the Triad (3) containing the beginning, the middle, and the end (Heaven, Earth, and Water). The Empress represents the original body, soul and spirit, which in old religions were feminine. These three were reshaped by the Christian religion to the masculine force of God, the father and the holy spirit. The Empress reclaims all three as feminine.

The Triangle shape is often related to the number 3 and the energies of the Universe. Many old religions believe in the Rule of 3 - that the energy you put out in the world is returned to you with 3 times the power. There are consequences to your actions, so be careful what kind of energy you put out there. The Empress guides you to express your creativity and produce growth. She gives you powerful positive energy to send out to the universe, to fulfill your destinies through the Law of 3.

As a symbol of creativity, the Empress can help you manifest positive, energizing thoughts and turn your desires into reality. She shows you how to develop your ideas, so you can build your life into joy and full of gratitude. When you express your desires and needs, the universe, through The Empress, responds and sends you the help you need to produce your greatest desires. But remember, The Empress doesn't force you; nor does she do all the work for you. You must take the first steps, engage yourself in the world and use your talents to move your desires into bloom. Once you do that, The Empress takes notice, bringing her gifts to you.

Don't mistake creative energy as just the artistic side of the world – writers, artists, actors, and others. Creative energy can be used in all manners and ways. Creativity can be expressed in starting a business, choosing a school, selecting a mate, cleaning out the garage, or gardening. Creativity exists in all of our everyday life tasks. The Empress tells you to enjoy your life as it vibrates its energy out into the world and to be full of gratitude. As the cycle of life continues, you are reminded that The Empress produces constant newness. New spring shoots and leaves, babies from all species, butterflies from cocoons; all come from The Empress.

CHAKRA

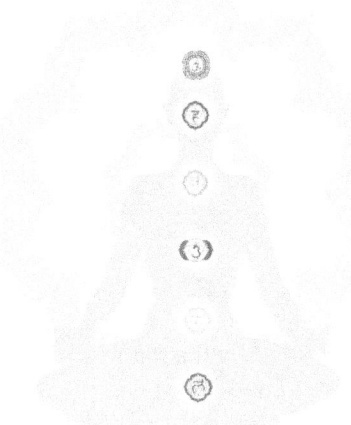

All seven chakras are related to The Empress. In some illustrations, the 7 pearls shown around the Empress's neck represent each of the body's 7 chakra centers. The orb the Empress holds is an indicator of spirit and wisdom.

The Empress is most often associated with the second Sacral Chakra, located 2 inches below the navel with a vibrant orange color. This chakra works with your reproductive system, the sexual organs, and the lumbar plexus; all energy areas that the Empress also oversees. These physical centers control and affect our creativity and desires. The Sacral Chakra in Sanskrit is "Svadhishthana," meaning abode, where you live. It is the literal core of your being and holds the 'real' you.

The Sacral Chakra is also paired with your sense of taste and appetite. It oversees both physical and spiritual wants. Connecting to your spirit, this chakra brings joy and fulfillment. Just as the Empress watches your well-being and prosperity, so does the Sacral Chakra bring you abundance, sexuality, and a feeling of joyful fullness. You create your life using this chakra. You create art, businesses, and babies. Through this encouragement, you open up and learn to live in the moment. If you shut this chakra down, you are closed off to the Empress gifts.

Associated with the psychology of our emotions and feelings, the Sacral chakra will guide your feelings about the world and your expression to others as you engage with them. It is not just lovers, but all people you relate with in the world, although it is central to your sexuality and sensuality. The sacral chakra rules your fantasies. Fantasies that the Empress often helps us create in the real world.

CORRESPONDENCES

- **Astrology:** Libra: ruled by the planets Venus and Jupiter.
- **Rune:** Inguz: gestation, internal growth, seed, fertility
- **I Ching:** Hexagram 29 Danger: This hexagram represents your soul. Be sincere and you will have success.
- **Symbol:** Triangle – the three-fold energies of the universe.
- **Animal:** Pelican
- **Element:** Earth

∼

READING CARD PLACEMENT

The Empress represents emotions and indicates the importance of following your instincts and feelings. Don't be misdirected by thought and action. Trust your intuition and your gut. She is abundant and full, waiting to give you the same abundance. You may be starting a new venture. The Empress brings healing for your emotional and physical wounds.

Past

When The Empress appears in the past, she indicates that she helped you with your last opportunity. This could be business, personal, or artistic. You may have ignored her efforts. Only the other cards in the layout will tell. It can indicate that action from the past requires nurturing to bring success into the present. The Empress may also represent a past feminine influence. This could be a role model, a relative, or someone whom you admire. This person greatly influenced you, and you will need to decide if their wisdom will serve you now or in the future.

Present

Placed in the present position, The Empress represents new beginnings. She brings fresh ideas and creativity for you to blossom. If you are currently unsatisfied with your life or aspects of it, changes are coming. The card can also indicate an older, experienced person who can guide you and assist with your new goals. While seeking your new life, remember the Empress represents giving, beauty and compassion, so pull those into your life. It is time to reap your harvest of past actions. Expect abundance. Be grateful for all you will receive. If you are starting a new project, The Empress signifies success.

Future

When the Empress appears in the future position, you are blessed. Her appearance is a good sign that whichever area of your life you are asking about, things will work out and grow in a positive manner.

YES / NO KEY INTERPRETATION

The Empress indicates positive productive opportunities to come. She tells you to move forward to fulfill your full potential. The answer you seek is yes.

KEYWORDS

Creativity, fertility, fulfilment, contentment, ideas, giving, compassion, prosperity, satisfaction, joy, happiness, beauty, abundance, Mother Earth.

5

THE EMPEROR

The Emperor represents male energy like your father, partner, and brother. He is a symbol of government and authority. The Emperor is shown sitting on a large stone throne, that is carved with four rams' heads representing his astrological sign, Aries, and holding in his right hand, a scepter with an ankh, the Egyptian symbol of life. In the emperor's left hand is an orb representing the world that he rules.

The long beard of The Emperor tells of his experience and wisdom. Through the years, he has learned much, including knowledge on how to rule and use power. He uses his authority and order for peace that benefits all. The crown on his head gives him authority, showing that he is in charge. A stern man, The Emperor controls his emotion using balance to bring others into his world of security.

In the distance, behind The Emperor's throne, are massive mountains illustrating his strength and foundation. A figure of authority and status, he shows you how authentic leadership works. The Emperor is the other half of The Empress, bringing male power into the world. Despite being male, he crosses genders, as does The Empress. Leadership, authority, self-discipline, and power pertain to all genders. His gender is not a mode of separateness but rather an inclusive process. The Emperor gives strength to those who carry the privilege and burden of leadership. He gives you an inner strength that you can rely on as you move through life to be the leader of your own life.

Wearing a red robe, he shows his passion for life and that despite his years, he has a large amount of energy. Under the robe, he wears a suit of armor, protecting him from attack. He is ready to fight if it is required and always on guard. In his world, there are rules and systems that all must follow. The Emperor dislikes chaos and disorder. Using his preference for regulations and guidelines, he ensures an ordered calm. Consider him the ultimate project manager. If there are problems, he asks you to reduce the issue down into pieces to find the order. Be strategic and organized. If you plan appropriately, you will be successful. With this kind of process, even if problems arise, you will be better prepared to take them on, turning them into success.

The Emperor has several names including:

- Charlemagne
- The Rebel
- Ulir
- Zeus

NUMBER 4 SYMBOLISM

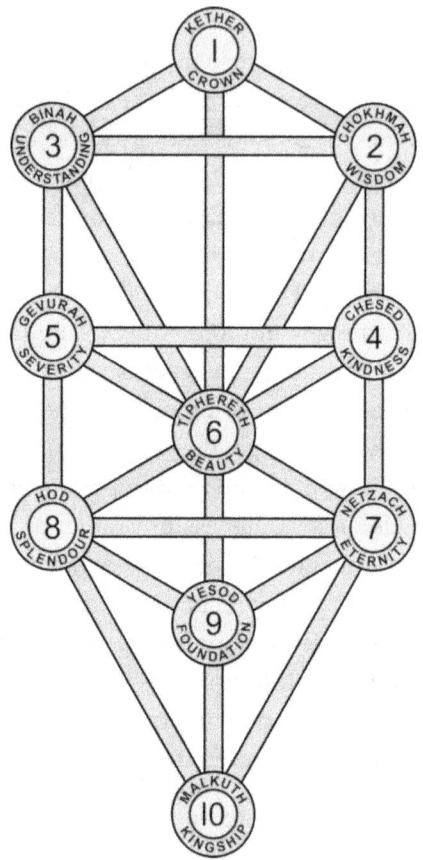

The Emperor's number is 4, a stable number. Four is a number of order and security. The number 4 is seen throughout the universe. There are 4 seasons, 4 directions and 4 elements: earth, water, air and fire. There are 4 corners in a square. The number 4 tells you to plan, to look ahead and be organized. As 4 creates order out of chaos, it is very suitable for The Emperor. The security of home is symbolized by the number 4. Number 4 is a number of the head and is often found ignoring the heart.

While 4 is a stable number, it also reminds you of the moon's 4 changing phases. Nothing in life remains static and in place. But like the moon, the phases of life are ordered and regular. As the cycle continues the full moon returns to our sight. Pythagoreans believe the number four, the Tetrad, to be a perfect number and a symbol of God.[1] They also believe there are 4 parts to the soul; mind, opinion, science and sense. All apply to The Emperor, for as stated above, The Emperor loves order. And science is our attempt at making sense and order of our universe.

The Emperor is on the 15th path of the Tree of Life, Samekh or Heh. Heh means window. Windows give you light, the ability to see the situation clearer and gain knowledge. An open window also provides fresh air, a new breath of life into your world. Heh is found between Tiphareth (Soul) and Yesod (Spiritual Realm). This path is considered difficult, requiring the experience of the Emperor to navigate.

Heh brings transparency to our actions and life. As you travel the 15th path, you know what you do and how you do it. You are also aware that others can see you. They see you for who you are, not the façade you present to the world. The purpose of this path is to give you light, only as much as you can handle, so you can make changes and improve yourself.

CHAKRA

An earth element, the Root Chakra, is the first chakra. The Sanskrit name for the root chakra is Muladhara, symbolized by a red lotus with four petals. The root chakra gives you the feeling of safety and a sense of being grounded. It's at the base of the spine and lays the foundation for expansion in your life. The first chakra is associated with security, your basic needs, and gives you the grounding for our life.

The Root Chakra, like The Emperor, brings you stability. But it is also instinctual. You don't need to think; it is part of who you are as a being. It is primal in nature. The Root Chakra rules your physical needs, such as food, water, and shelter. Think of Maslov's hierarchy of needs. One can't function well in life unless these basic needs are first met. It also warns us of danger, both physical and psychological. Red is a warning color and The Root Chakra instinctively kicks in when it feels we are encountering difficulties.

The root chakra, when balanced, creates the foundation of security. It is the foundation on which we build our life and allows us to feel safe as we explore our universe. Like The Emperor card, the root chakra gives us wisdom. It provides your ability to trust while you are out in the world.

This chakra oversees your sexuality and the urge to procreate. When the Root Chakra is balanced, the energy flows, and you feel secure and trusting. We can then use The Emperor's guidance and leadership to plan for our goals and dreams.

CORRESPONDENCES

- **Astrology:** Scorpio: leaders, pioneers, initiate rather than complete
- **Rune:** Thurisaz: force, conflict, destruction
- **I Ching:** Hexagram 14 Ta Yu: The Great Possessor. Predicts great wealth and success
- **Symbol:** The Ankh cross
- **Animal:** Ram
- **Element:** Fire

READING CARD PLACEMENT

The Emperor represents a strategic thinker who sets out plans and creates order out of chaos. A symbol of the masculine energy within us all, he creates structure and rules. The Emperor dispenses knowledge and guidance with grace and firmness. A rational man, he wants what is right for all. The Emperor brings order, discipline and improvement to your life. When The Emperor appears for you, it can indicate that you will gain status or that help comes from someone who has a higher position than you. Generally, the Emperor works in the career and business area of your life.

Past

Previously, an authority figure, such as a boss or mentor, played a role in shaping your life. They gave you rules and gently guided you to the correct path in life. This allowed you to progress and is part of why you are where you are now in the world. If you rebelled against these rules and authority you may need to catch up and integrate their teachings in the present. This card can also indicate that a conflict is ended, and you are moving on from it.

Present

The law is on your side and you have moral authority on your side. Someone in a position of authority could be influencing you. This person could be in a leadership role in your life, or it could be someone you admire from afar or in a book. You are gaining skills and the confidence to continue on your path, learning, and growing. You could take on a leadership role but if so, remember The Emperor's guidance and knowledge. Don't let it go to your head. Be a fair leader. Create a vision and bring others along who can see what you have planned. Listen to advice and remember that smart leaders surround themselves with smarter and more skilled people than they are in the work.

Future

Use your leadership skills to move forward into stability. Remember The Emperor's guidance and knowledge because you will own all your decisions. Be wise and clear. Create a plan, be realistic and orderly. All will go well if you use the skills you've gained to be fair and transparent with those around you.

YES / NO KEY INTERPRETATION

Use The Emperor's stability and rational approach to take control of your life. Your answer is yes.

KEYWORDS

Leadership, Authority, Stability, Rules, Planning.

6
THE HIEROPHANT

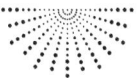

The Hierophant is the masculine based counterpart to the High Priestess. He sits between two pillars in a sacred temple wearing a robe of red, blue and white. A tiered crown sits on his head, representing the three worlds the Hierophant rules: the conscious, unconscious, and super-conscious. The black 'W' on the crown's top is the Hebrew Letter Vav, meaning nail or hook.

Unlike the High Priestess card, there is no veil connecting the two pillars behind The Hierophant. The empty space between The Hierophant's pillars shows that he is open to sharing his expertise with all who wish to learn. And that behind him, the knowledge is endless.

The Hierophant is a conservative man. In his left hand he holds the Papal Cross, a triple sceptre. His right hand is raised in a traditional Christian blessing, with two fingers pointing to the sky and two pointing to the earth. Representing religious leaders is a solemn affair and the Hierophant takes his role seriously. He must explain the mysteries of the universe which can be a large weight on his soul.

Two men kneel before him, their heads shaved in the way of a traditional monk. The Hierophant's desire is to dispense his wisdom to everyone open to hearing it. The Hierophant guides those who seek him out into his mysteries. At the Hierophant's feet are crossed keys representing his ability to unlock those mysteries. When the Hierophant appears in your reading, traditional morality and values are brought to light and playing a role in your life. The traditions could be those created by your family, religion, or culture. It also speaks of your reliance on others to know the right way instead of having an inner individualistic guide. The Hierophant symbolizes spiritual rituals such as confirmation, bar mitzva, marriage, or baptism. His appearance can also predict that you will meet a wise person who can provide knowledge pertinent to you at this moment.

The Hierophant is guiding you to stay on the well-trod path for now. This is not the time to rebel or seek non-traditional methods.

The Hierophant means many different things but often refers to your emotional and spiritual development. The Hierophant provides teaching and guidance from a very traditional perspective. He can be authoritative and rigid in his advice. If you meditate on the Hierophant, he shows you the path towards fulfillment. The way forward may include many things; joining a group, finding the right book to guide you, or taking a class. Each path is different.

Other names for the Hierophant are:

- The High Priest
- The Pope
- The Magus
- Osirus

NUMBER 5 SYMBOLISM

The Hierophant's number is 5, which is often associated with Hermes and Mercury. Number 5 symbolizes the balance between your spirituality and the physical side of life. The Mayans considered 5 a symbol of perfection. It brings adaptability and balance to your life, especially between your desire for material things and your spirit. The number 5 brings change to your life, and opportunities will be appearing when the Hierophant shows in a reading.

Everywhere you look in the world, 5 is there. You have 5 fingers on each hand, 5 toes on each foot. There are 5 books in the Torah and 5 pillars of Islam. On the cross, Jesus had 5 wounds called the 5 Holy Wounds.

The pentagram contains 5 points and, in some faiths, is considered magical. The upward point is spirit. The other 4 points are representative of the 4 elements: earth, air, fire, and water. The number 5 is seen as mystical, almost magical. Associated with Mars, it can mean conflict and war. Peace can come from war, and sometimes a struggle is needed to sort through the chaos and get to the place where peace can reside.

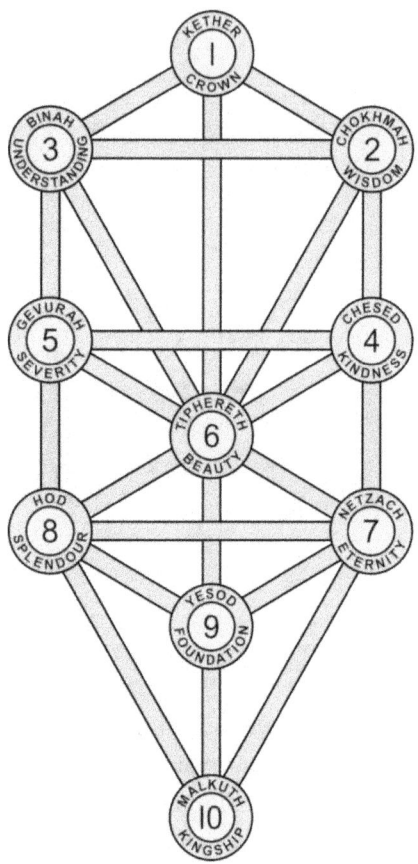

The Hierophant is located on the 16th path (Ayin, meaning eye) in the Tree of Life, between Tipareth and Hod. The path joins Chokmah (Victory) and Chesed (Splendor) and reaches the right and left pillars. The 16th path shows us hidden ways we keep from ourselves and the world. You learn to recognize the truth and dismiss the illusions that can keep you bound. All the false 'truths' that you have accumulated over the years get swept away. This can be difficult. We all cling to our beliefs, no matter how outdated or wrong they are proven to be. Enter the fire with determination and allow the flames to cleanse you.

You will gather strength. You will learn truths that are solid and a base to build your life on.

CHAKRA

Like The Magician, The Hierophant is associated with the Throat chakra. The Throat chakra, when balanced, provides peace, joy, and emotional harmony along with determination. The Throat chakra is related to sound as it is through the throat that sound comes from us. The sound vibrates throughout your body and is one of the main ways you learn to communicate and express yourself. It is why music is healing and the vibrations of a brass bowl echo through your body.

The Throat chakra is called Vishuddha, meaning pure. Located at the center of the neck on the throat, the Throat chakra is symbolized with sixteen purple/blue petals. The petals are shiny like a reflection in a pool of water. The energies associated with the Throat chakra include communication, creativity, expression, and the realization of your truth.

The Throat chakra is about the expression of yourself: Your truth, purpose in life, creativity. Note that this chakra has a natural connection with the second chakra or sacral chakra, the center of emotions and creativity. The throat chakra's emphasis is on expressing and projecting the creativity into the world, according to its perfect form or authenticity. With The Hierophant, the Throat Chakra expresses a traditional viewpoint, views that have existed in the universe for centuries.

The Throat Chakra also connects you to the spirits and our intuitive abilities. The Throat chakra, like The Hierophant, aids you in creating your visions and then taking them into reality. When your Throat Chakra is blocked, you may find it challenging to bring your purpose to life or to find the perfect career path. When you vocalize your plans, the universe hears and sends help to you in various forms.

Because of its connection to spirit and intuition, opening the Throat chakra can realign your energies and allow your intuition to flourish once again. It can allow you to speak your truth. Not what others want to hear, but what is true for you. When The Hierophant appears in your reading, it is showing you that at this time, following traditions will aid you in bringing forth your voice.

CORRESPONDENCES

- **Astrology:** Taurus. Love physical pleasures, excess,
- comfort
- **Rune:** Raidho (Chariot, travel):
- **I Ching:** Hexagram 11 Tai: Peace or Harmony. Small issues will disappear, and great fortune and success will appear
- **Symbol:** Keys of Wisdom
- **Animal:** Bull
- **Element:** Earth

READING CARD PLACEMENT

When the Hierophant appears in a reading, it is time to embrace the conventional and stick to traditional ways. Instead of being innovative, adapt to beliefs and systems which already exist. It is not the time to introduce radical change in your life. Keep your passions and desires but use caution. Take advice and don't rush. Look for clues in the cards that surround the Hierophant in the reading.

Past

Your past projects gave you valuable insight and experience. The traditions served you well and now you must consider if you will continue on their path or find a different way.

Present

For the moment follow a traditional path, don't go it alone. You may be presented with a teacher or mentor who can teach you many things. Accept what they have to offer and learn their wisdom. Let others into your life. Seek out a wise person to guide you.

Future

You may have been walking your own independent way, but the time is coming for you to follow a traditional path. To achieve success, seek out those who are more knowledgeable than you. Live your truth within the traditional boundaries. Be honorable. Look for a role model who has spiritual depth.

YES / NO INTERPRETATION

As a strong symbol of tradition, the Hierophant gives guidance and advice. He asks that you seek advice from traditional sources; a mentor, religious leader, those with wisdom. The answer is maybe. Talk to wise people.

KEYWORDS

Spiritual wisdom, religion, conformity, tradition, dogma, morality, values

7

THE LOVERS

The Lovers card presents a naked man and woman standing beneath the angel Raphael. Raphael is the angel of air and a Gemini astrology sign. Associated with mental activity and speech, the Lovers card brings the foundations for healthy relationships.

The couple happily stands in the fertile Garden of Eden. Behind the woman is a fruit tree, the Tree of Knowledge, with a snake entwined around the trunk, reminding us of temptation and the impacts on your life if you are unable to resist. Knowledge brings understanding but also suffering. Behind the man is a tree of flames, believed to be the tree of life, representing passion and desire. The twelve flames symbolize time and eternity. They are reaching up to God. Thus, the choice between God and suffering.

The ground is a bright spring green with a mountain rising in the distance into a blue sky between the couple. The volcanic mountain in the background, on occasion, erupts with passion.

In the middle of the card, an angel sits on a full white pillow of a cloud, wearing a purple cloak. Lifting its hands in blessing, the angel's face is a golden yellow that matches the sunshine that floods the card. The couple is happy because Raphael blesses them. Some believe that the couple are Adam and Eve, representing mind and rationality vs heart and emotion. When confronting a decision, often you are making the choice between these two areas.

Raphael, the Angel, represents spirit and spirituality, your ability to grow and become aware of how you want to move through the world. The woman looks up to the Angel, wanting to learn from him but with her feet firmly planted on the ground. The man looks over at the woman with desire, showing you your unconscious desires. Your unconscious knows what you desire and your true path in life. The Lover's card brings those desires to the light, helping you work towards fulfilling them.

Depending on your question and the placement of the card, The Lovers card can mean choice. Just as Eve made a choice in the garden, the Lovers card tells you that your choices can lead you down different roads in life, and you need to consider all possible outcomes to make the best decision for your life at this moment. Sensual pleasures (for example romantic love, materialism) can take your focus away from the longer-term perspective, causing you to make a negative decision. Or one that takes you away from your true path. A correct decision may be difficult to comprehend, so take the time to meditate and examine all the options. A positive outcome is possible with thought and planning.

The Lovers card might also be telling you that it is time to examine your values. What do you believe, and what are you willing to stand up for? You should re-examine your values regularly to ensure they still serve you and are aligned to who you are today. When making choices or deciding to commit to a relationship, knowing who you are and what is essential to you will guide you as you navigate the choices the universe presents to you. If you don't know who you are, you can't find your true path, nor can you join with another in honesty.

The Lovers is a card that speaks of honesty and communication between people: lovers, friends, and colleagues. The man and woman are naked and exposed, vulnerable to each other and the world. The card is telling you that to have good relationships, you must learn to open your heart to others and share who you are with trust and confidence. When you do this, it creates a powerful bond between you and those you care about. It is the only way to create a strong, fulfilling relationship.

Other names of The Lover's card include:

- Marriage
- The Brothers
- The Twins

NUMBER 6 SYMBOLISM

The Lovers card is the 6th card in the Major Arcana. The number 6 represents the act of giving and receiving and illustrates the difference between giving and receiving. It represents the relationship between your conscious self and your unconscious, which combine to create who you are and what you choose. Number 6 also represents Gemini and the dual nature of the twins. Like everyone in the world, you have polarities, opposite sides that pull at you. Knowing your true self and your values let you deal with these polarities and ensure they are aligned with your values.

The Hebrew letter for the Lovers card is Zain, which means sword. A sword cuts both ways and can make sharp divisions, allowing us to work with our dual nature. As The Lovers card deals with decisions, a sword will help cut through the maze and make the path ahead clear. As long as you only deal with your conscious thoughts, you cannot gain true knowledge and where you desire to go. Digging deep into your unconscious allows you to uncover who you are and which path you need to walk.

The Lovers card path 16 is near the top of the Tree of Life. The path, Zain, runs from Binah (understanding and truth) to Tiphareth (beauty/harmony). When you travel Zain, you become the sword, capable of seeing both sides of a situation and cutting through the noise to find the truth of the matter. This is a way for those who give selflessly and give hope to others.

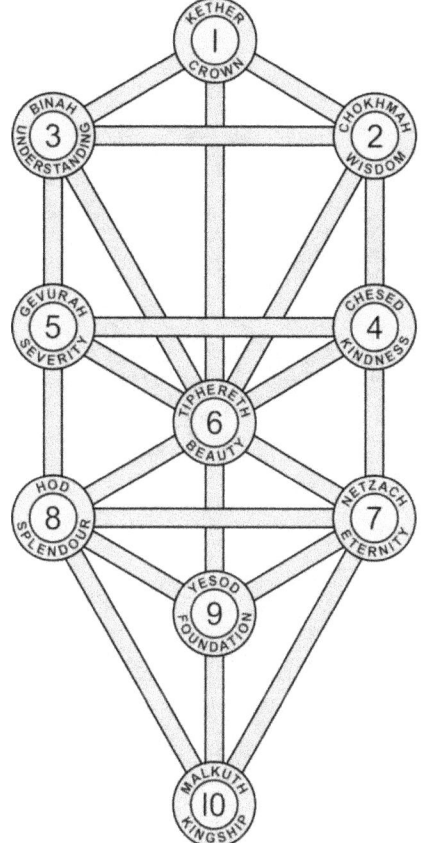

Zain also combines the opposites into one, creating a whole. Polarity pieces, like male and female, merge into one, becoming a new consciousness. Using The Lovers, you are able to have great insight and understanding as you follow this path.

CHAKRA

The heart chakra is positioned in the center of your chest, to the right of your heart. In Sanskrit, it's name is Anahata (unstruck); it creates your capacity for compassion, openness, affection, and love. Colored green, it is considered the 4th energy center, bridging your earthly desires with the spiritual and represented by two triangles forming a 6-pointed star in a circle with 12 petals. The triangles represent the element of air and the union of opposites - male and female, earth and spirit. Like The Lovers, the heart chakra is seeking to open you to your polarities and bring the opposites into harmony and balance.

This chakra works with The Lovers card to harmonize your relationships, create empathy and compassion for others, and help you change and move forward in peace. It also pulls in the spiritual elements, as does The Lovers card, through the angel, Raphael.

Just as number 6 is about giving and receiving, so is the heart chakra. Working with The Lovers, the 3 combine to teach you about connections, relationships and being open. These 3 want you to love yourself and, through that process, love others. Be open to receiving the gift of love from others. This is love from and to all others, not just romantic love.

The heart chakra helps us see the beauty in the world. It is what leaves us awestruck when we stand in front of an amazing work of art like Botticelli's The Birth of Venus. Or when we stop to admire a beautiful garden instead of just striding on by. Or love a wrinkled, old man as if we were looking at a newborn. We see the beauty and our hearts blossom.

CORRESPONDENCES

- **Astrology:** Gemini: the twins. Ruled by Mercury and Venus
- **Rune:** Gebo: love, partnership
- **I Ching:** Hexagram 19 Lin: Approach. Spring is approaching after a dark winter. This hexagram provides hope and success
- **Symbol:** Five-Pointed Star
- **Animal:** Swan
- **Element:** Air

∽

READING CARD PLACEMENT

The Lovers card is teaching you about meaningful relationships and decisions. In a Tarot reading, it may be describing a love relationship, romantic, friendship, or family. Or a personal passion; a hobby, work, or other past time.

The Lovers is a card of duality in love and creating harmony. The Lovers illustrated have trust and a strong bond. It is also a card of choice and making clear decisions.

Past

A conflict was resolved, or a difficult decision was made and set the path for your future life. You made the right decision. Your foundations are strong. You may have joined with another person and created a new relationship or strengthened an old relationship.

Present

Placed in the present position, The Lovers indicate that you are currently involved in a strong relationship or have a strong desire for someone. Or a passion that you love is underway. If you are already in a relationship, the card tells you that it is strong and something you can build on.

Depending on the cards surrounding The Lovers, the meaning can also be that you have a decision to make. You must use the sword to cut through all the meaningless weeds surrounding this decision and come to the core. For whatever decision you make will impact your life. Choose carefully. Your decision must align with your values and beliefs, or it will create difficulty for you down the road.

Future

Placed in the future, the card suggests that a strong relationship is coming that will benefit you. It may also indicate that you will need to make choices in the future, and you must prepare yourself now so you will make the correct decision. Decisions are often not easy, with each path giving you an equal but different outcome. Meditate on your values and where you would like your life's path to take you.

YES / NO KEY INTERPRETATION

The answer is yes. Follow your intuition and heart.

KEYWORDS

Love, relationships, sex, values, good decisions, choices.

8

THE CHARIOT

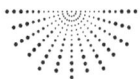

The Chariot Tarot card depicts a warrior king standing tall with shoulders back, inside a chariot pulled by two black and white sphinxes. The sphinxes show the duality of nature, the positive and negative aspects of life, and your opposite personalities. They also illustrate the foreign land from which the warrior king is returning, having conquered his enemy. Sphinxes tie the Tarot to Egyptian mythology.

The sphinx is an animal with the head of a woman, the body of a lioness, the wings of an eagle, and a serpent's tail. The sphinx was the ruler of Thebes' city, where travelers to the city would have to answer a riddle before they could enter. If they did not give the correct answer, the sphinx would kill and eat them. The riddle was, "What goes on fours in the morning, on twos in the afternoon, and on threes at night?" When Oedipus, a Greek king, traveled to Thebes, the sphinx asked him the riddle. His answer was 'it is a human being'; a human being walks on all fours in early life, on two legs as an adult, and with a walking stick in old age. The fact that the warrior king has tamed these sphinxes tells you of his strength.

The warrior king's armor is decorated with crescent moons showing his spiritual influence and connections. The star crown gives him spiritual and physical enlightenment. The laurel wreath on his head, confirms his victory. Sewn-on his chest is a square, illustrating the element of earth, grounding him. His gold belt is adorned with astrological symbols. On the front of his chariot is a winged shield.

The charioteer doesn't grasp reins to lead the sphinxes but instead holds a scepter through which he controls the chariot using his strength of will. The sphinxes are pulling in opposite directions, but he still manages them, forcing them to the road he wishes to take. Like the sphinxes, you also have opposite desires that, on occasion, pull you in two different directions. But if you control the reins, that is your emotions and willpower, then you succeed.

Over his head is a blue canopy covered with six-pointed stars, revealing that he works with the celestial world and the Divine. Behind the chariot is a river symbolizing life and emotions, that moves with a natural flow. There is also a walled city. He is riding in triumph, returning from a victory over evil forces. And even though he is returning victorious, he is ready for action, should it be needed.

The Chariot has many names:

- Horus
- Sun God
- The Centurion
- Victory

NUMBER 7 SYMBOLISM

The Chariot is the 7th card in the Major Arcana. The number 7 represents the force of action that can be used to reach a successful conclusion. It also brings happiness, symbolizing positive matters, including renewal and perfection. As the number 7 is perfection and security, it represents earthly and divine harmony. Some believe that 7 is so perfect and powerful that it is a connection to the universe. It is considered a sacred number in several traditions, for example, Christianity. In the Christian tradition, 7 is a number of perfection, as in the book of Genesis creation was completed in 7 days.

There are 7 days in a week, and the Sabbath is on the 7th day. There are 7 colors in the rainbow. There were 7 wonders of the world: the Great Pyramid of Giza, the Hanging Gardens of Babylon, the Temple of Artemis at Ephesus, the Statue of Zeus at Olympia, the Mausoleum at Halicarnassus, the Colossus of Rhodes, and the Lighthouse of Alexandria. Jackpots in gambling machines display three 7's to indicate a win.

Mythical legends gave the seventh son of a seventh son magical powers and status. Seven is a prime number. Seven is considered a sacred number and spiritual in nature.

On the tree of life, the Chariot is on the 18th path, Cheth meaning Fence. Cheth travels from Binah (understanding) to Geburah. It represents the start of new activities or goals and the hope of success.

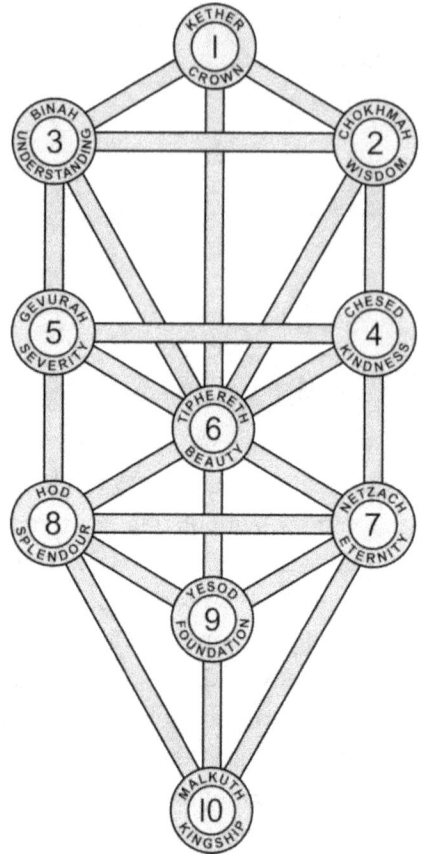

From Binah to the grounded Geburah, your dreams are moved from thought to creation. Connected to Mars, a symbol of war, it is something the Chariot understands well. This is a profound path that speaks of self-control and self-will, also conquered by the warrior king. Some people believe the Chariot carries the souls of the dead to a higher plane and is the gateway to understanding.

CHAKRA

The Chariot is associated with the third chakra, the Solar Plexus chakra, Manipura, meaning shining gem. Located in the solar plexus area, near your diaphragm, it is the 3rd chakra from the bottom. It is illustrated by a golden yellow circle with 10 petals. In the middle is a triangle pointing down. As does The Chariot tarot card, it deals with your willpower and a sense of purpose in the world.

It also works with our ego. Working with this chakra, you can move into action and meet your challenges to move forward. And like The Chariot, this chakra requires balance especially balance in exerting your power, in your emotions and in dealing with the people around you. Power doesn't mean power over others. Real power shows your ability to control your thoughts and emotions, using them in positive life enhancing ways.

Your Solar Plexus chakra is working whenever you exert self-control. You are channeling the warrior king of the Chariot card. Use his energy to gain courage. If you are fearful of a situation, adopt his posture; head held high, shoulders back, deep breaths. You will activate the Solar Plexus chakra, and it will assist you in your challenge.

The Solar Plexus chakra aids you in following your true path and remembering your values. It also helps you have an awareness of the world around you and guard against those things that can pull you away from your values and beliefs. Your ability to achieve your goals is held in the Solar Plexus chakra.

CORRESPONDENCES

- **Astrology:** Cancer: emotional, intuitive, ruled by the moon, creative
- **Rune:** Kenaz: power to create your own reality, the power of light. Open to new energy
- **I Ching:** Hexagram 34 Ta Chuang: Great Power. Use your inner strength to go forward and achieve success
- **Symbol:** The Moon
- **Animal:** Sphinx
- **Element:** Water

~

READING CARD PLACEMENT

When the Chariot card appears in a Tarot reading, you are working towards victory. Appreciate that all the struggles and obstacles are leading you to where you need to be. When you reach there, you will enter your new life with the same air as the warrior king on The Chariot card. Triumphant, proud, and in control. The Chariot card tells you that you can control your life – belief systems, your thoughts, and emotions. The Chariot can indicate an essential and successful journey that you are about to undertake. Take hold of the reins and guide your chariot to your goal and destination. You will have to work to attain your goal. There is no free ride here. Holding the chariot firm and moving in the right direction can be difficult, both physically and psychologically. The Chariot card tells you that this journey you are taking will be hard work, and it may take a while to achieve your goal. This isn't an instant win time. You may experience setbacks but remind yourself that this is a learning journey. As long as you use the wisdom of the Chariot and control your ego, you will be successful. Use your control, and victory is yours.

Past

You have been through struggles, some of which are of your own making. You have learned and in the process your strength has grown. You are ready to move forward with your new-found knowledge and understanding.

Present

You are on the right path and will overcome all obstacles in a decisive victory. Focus on your goals and what you are attaining, but also enjoy the journey on your way to success.

Future

The goals will be achieved if you let go of your ego. Achievement, honor and recognition are all possible outcomes for you if you hold fast and guide your actions.

YES / NO KEY INTERPRETATION

Yes. Take charge and go for it. It could also be the final success you have been working towards.

KEYWORDS

Victory, self-confidence, skill, progress, obstacles, balance, control.

9

STRENGTH

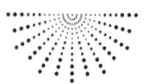

The Strength Tarot card's image depicts a woman, in a white robe, holding the lower jaw of a lion up while she gently pushes its head down to close the jaw. Although the lion could readily turn and harm her, the woman has tamed his wildness using love and strength.

The lion symbolizes your passion and desires. By taming the lion, the woman lets you know that your fundamental nature and instinctive desires can also be tamed. Not eradicated but used in positive ways. Learning how to use your strength and remain calm allows you to evaluate situations against your values and the outcomes before taking action that might be disastrous.

The woman isn't using force to close the lion's jaw; she uses her strength gained through self-control and knowledge. She has no desire to kill or harm the lion; rather she wishes it to work for her when she needs or feels safe to unleash it.

Wearing a white robe, the woman shows her purity. Her face is caring and loving. She is not taming the lion for evil purposes or to hold it in a cage but to show it the joy of balance. Above her, the infinity symbol hangs, a sign of infinite knowledge and wisdom, an equalizer against the lion's passion and cravings.

The blue mountains illustrate a strong foundation and the stability created from that calmness. Yellow sunlight floods the background, giving warmth, and contributing to a sense of calm and strength. Lions are a symbol of courage and passion. Both are necessary for survival and joy in your life. You need courage to start to walk, create a relationship, fall in love and bring joy to the human experience. But courage and passion can easily be misused or directed to the wrong pursuit and need to be developed to be used in the best manner. Without a checkpoint, courage, desire, and passion can lead to your destruction.

Strength is power. This is a positive card on many levels, from the physical to the psychological. Strength can be used to improve your life, or it can be a negative force. The strength to face your demons is imperative, but taking your strength and using it to cause harm to others will cause pain, not only for the others, but eventually for you. Strength helps you face your problems with perseverance and will.

Alistair Crowley called the card Lust with the woman riding the lion, another illustration of taming your desires.

The Strength card is also known as:

- Fortitude
- Lust

NUMBER 8 SYMBOLISM

Strength's card number is 8 and is the foundation of the other 8 cards in the deck. The number 8 represents balance with the ability to both create and destroy. Eight balances your material desires with your material wishes. Like infinity, 8 is a perfect number complete unto itself. Turn the number 8 onto its side, and you have the infinity symbol.

In the Bible, 8 signifies resurrection as the number of a new beginning. In China the number 8 is believed to express the totality of the universe and considered a lucky number. The number 8 is often associated with wealth and prosperity. The Pythagoreans called the number 8 Ogdoad and considered it a holy number.

Number 8 symbolizes abundance and power and deals with career, business, and authority. Like the Strength card, the number 8 balances out your life. It can both create and destroy. As in Strength, it balances the material with the spiritual. And although it deals with abundance, your abundance may not come in the form of money but rather emotional and spiritual gifts.

On the Tree of Life, Strength is located between Geburah (known as

Strength), on the Pillar of Severity and Chesed, on the Pillar of Mercy, the 19th pathway, Teth, meaning serpent. Geburah represents strength through established foundations, using your will and power. This is a balancing path and with Geburah, where you find solutions to problems and overcome obstacles.

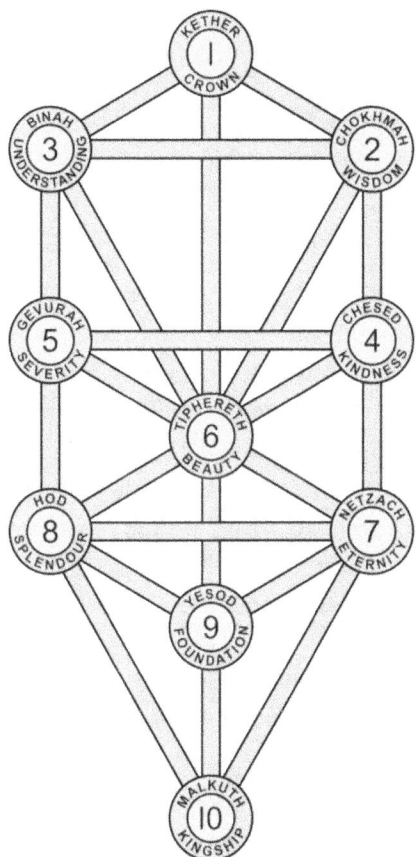

You learn to keep peaceful through your inner strength. Chesed shows us how to expand with strong foundations. This expansion can represent retirement, revitalization, and recuperation. It is a place where you can learn how to wield your strength in harmony with the creation of your reality. It can bring ecstasy and give you the ability to dance your way through life. Too much strength can cause pain, too little and you are weak.

CHAKRA

Anahata or Heart Chakra is the 4th chakra, according to Hindu tradition. In Sanskrit, Anahata means unhurt, unstruck, or unbeaten.

Anahata moves love through your life, creating connections with others. It enhances compassion and caring. The heart chakra encourages you to see people positively and enjoy their goodness. You can acknowledge their flaws, but still care for them, as you also see their greatness. Anahata brings completeness to life. Through the heart chakra, much is healed, and much good is done. The Strength card helps you understand that you gain strength through your heart, not from your physical abilities. It comes from your inner soul, from love.

Located in the center of your chest, the Heart chakra is the 4th chakra, symbolized by a green 6-pointed star in a circle with 12 petals. The heart chakra helps you love both yourself and others. It involves you in relationships, which allows you to grow. You change as you allow yourself to experience empathy and gather insights through these relationships.

Anahata energy shows you that you are part of the universe. That all of us are interconnected and there is a greater whole. Carl Jung defined the collective unconscious as a part of our mind that is connected to the whole of the universe. The heart chakra guides you from that collective unconscious, allowing you to vibrate with the universe and feel connected.

The Heart Chakra grants you this universal knowledge as it guides you to love not only yourself but others. It transforms you and gives insight to yourself and those around you. This is the Strength that the tarot card guides you too.

CORRESPONDENCE

- **Astrology:** Leo. Self-confident, charismatic, fun, resilient, generous
- **Rune:** Wunjo: joy and fellowship
- **I Ching:** Hexagram 34 Great Power Use your inner strength to go forward and achieve success
- **Symbol:** Lion
- **Animal:** Lion
- **Element:** Fire

READING CARD PLACEMENT

Follow your higher purpose and turn to your intuition and values for guidance. Use your intuition to develop your character. Use grace and have patience. Don't try to force anything or anyone. If you find yourself pushing, it probably isn't meant to be. If problems arise, stay calm and meditate on the best actions to take to resolve the issue.

Past

You had concerns and issues, but you faced them with patience, relying on your inner strength. The other cards in the layout show if you overcame or if the problem is still with you. You balanced all and kept your faith.

Present

Remain calm and use your inner strength to guide you. If there are struggles, be compassionate as you work to resolve issues. Use patience and your intuition to guide you. Remember that you are connected to all in the universe and that the universe wants to serve you. Don't let your emotions or impulsive actions run your life, instead take command and use your strength for the greater good.

Future

You have the strength to grow and learn. Any obstacles that arrive, you will handle them. Improvements can come provided you use patience and remember your connection to the universe. Grab onto any opportunities, breath deep, and remember your strength will guide you.

YES / NO KEY INTERPRETATION

Yes, if you use your strength wisely. Have patience, it may not come immediately.

KEYWORDS

Compassion, patience, vitality, will power.

10

THE HERMIT

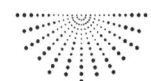

The Hermit card is a dark winter card. It exudes cold. Holding a lantern, an old man shines a light of wisdom for those stumbling around in the cold and darkness. He stands in snow on the top of a mountain, against a bleak background bracing himself with a staff, displaying his power to the world.

At the apex of his life, the Hermit has achieved knowledge and success, including spiritual awareness and depth. Now that he has experience of the world and its inhabitants, he has no need of company. But he is still willing to speak to all who venture to find him. The Hermit is committed to his path and aware of all the follies he may encounter along the way. Inside the lantern is a 6-pointed star known as the Seal of Solomon, or the Star of David, symbolic of wisdom. The Hermit has retreated from life and spends his time meditating and learning to enhance his earthly knowledge and expand his spiritual truth.

The Hermit represents the seeker of knowledge abiding within you. He is the gut feeling that guides you along the path: your intuition, your unconscious. A lonely night wanderer, The Hermit searches for knowledge that can only be found by looking inward and listening to your intuition and your soul. To hear his inner voice, he silences the external and questions his material desires, which loudly try to interfere with his meditations. His purpose is to find the truth and the peace that can only come from living your true self. This is not time to rely on others input. It is time to shine your own light.

The Hermit asks you to forget about your past; the old hurts and concerns of yesterday. If you can't let go, you will impact your current relationships, work, or creative projects. It is time to move from the shadows into the light. Clear out negative energies and release them into the wind. You can have memories; you can learn from the past, but who you are today is not dependent on who you were yesterday or who you will be tomorrow.

The Hermit holds his lantern, lighting his way and reminding you that the answers you seek will come from within you. Be honest with yourself, and you will find your way to a blue sky in the daylight. A bright and cloudless future awaits you unless you refuse to stop for reflection, meditation and solitude. Schedule time to ask yourself if you are still on the right path. Do your partners, lovers, and friends reflect your values? Do you love your career? It doesn't have to be perfect. Remember the 80/20 rule; your work, relationships, and creative projects should be 80% positive and fulfilling, with 20% allowing for times when it doesn't provide you with joy.

The Hermit is standing on snow. The cold keeps you alert and aware. To evaluate your life, you need to look at things with a calm, objective eye. The Hermit asks you to go deep, beyond a cursory evaluation. Spring will come when you take the time to dig deep and look at what you have planted. You must do this by yourself to ensure that your desires and reflections are based on your analysis, needs, and values. Retreat from others and allow yourself the gift of alone time. Turn off the tv and computer. Leave your phone in a drawer. Be alone. If you do this contemplation with others, their desires and values will influence your thoughts and outcomes. Knowledge will come when you remove all distractions and allow yourself to find out who you really are and where you want to go in this life.

For some people, the silence of the Hermit is disturbing. They want the noise, the interactions and will do anything to avoid being alone and in silence. But the wisdom you will receive on this path is worth pushing through your fear of aloneness. Always remember that you are choosing this path; it is not being imposed on you. You can leave the silence at any time, but the Hermit asks that you stay long enough to receive your inner knowledge and understand your reflections.

The Hermit represents the wisdom that comes with old age. But you don't have to be old to obtain what he has, especially if you seek out knowledge from others who have already trod a path. Mentors and role models can assist you. But remember, you know yourself best, and even a small twist in values can lead you down the wrong path. Read, listen, watch but always remove yourself to reflect and evaluate. Never adopt something without long reflection on how this truly integrates with your values.

Other names for the Hermit card are:

- Lamp of Truth

- Le Moine ("The Monk")
- Shaman
- Time
- The Sage
- Cronus
- Heimdallr
- Saint Frances

NUMBER 9 SYMBOLISM

The Hermit is the 9th card in the Major Arcana. In numerology, the number 9 is the judgement number and speaks of a time of evaluation. Number 9 is a number that goes into itself, just as the Hermit encourages you to do when he asks for self-reflection and looking inward to seek the answers. The number 9 moves you from the abstract to the concrete.

A spiritual number, 9 represents the purpose of your life. There are many cultures and religions where 9 is considered meaningful. The Chinese consider 9 good luck as it sounds like the Chinese word for long life. Chinese mythology gives the dragon 9 lives. In western culture, cats have 9 lives. In ancient Egypt, there were 9 gods; in Greek mythology, there were 9 muses.

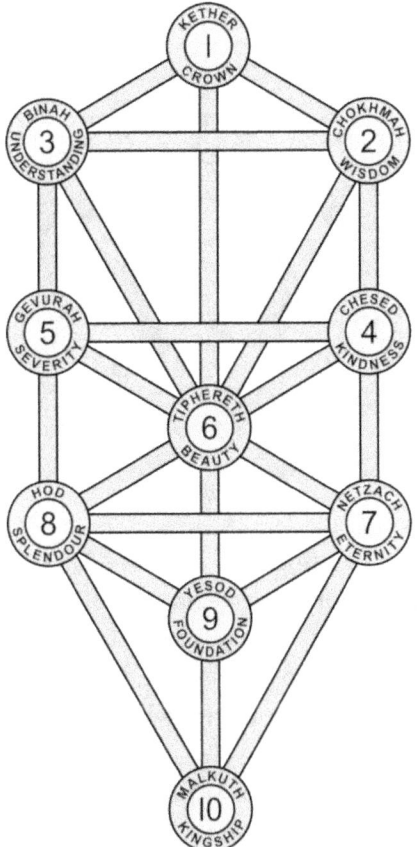

The Hermit is associated with the Path of Yod, the twentieth path in the Tree of Life. In the Tree of Life, this path runs from Chesed to Tiphereth, symbolized by an open hand. The path is related to wisdom and secret knowledge. You must walk this path by yourself to gain understanding, just as the Hermit walks alone.

CHAKRA

The Hermit card is associated with the Third Eye chakra, called Ajna in Sanscrit, meaning perception. Located on the forehead, between the eyebrows, the Third Eye is the center of intuition, openness and imagination. Indigo in color, the Chakra symbol is composed of 2 petals of the lotus flower with a white circle enclosing a triangle and the symbol for OM.

This chakra is the combination of all the elements in their pure form. The Third Eye chakra is the link between your mind and the outer world. It gives you clarity and self-reflection, allowing you to hear your inner voice and understand what you already know. The Third-Eye chakra helps you see through the illusions that the world and others present to you. The clarity of vision helps you see beyond the words presented to you and understand the speaker's true intentions. You become mindful. Don't mistake this for cynicism or skepticism, for it is true wisdom that allows you to cut through the veil and see the truth.

You can often be presented with an issue that is neither right nor wrong. It just is; it is suitable for some and wrong for others. The Third Eye chakra, along with the Hermit, allows you to understand this and see that even though others may benefit from an idea or belief, it is not for you. Nothing in this world is 100% right for all people (maybe drinking water), nor is something continually right.

What worked for you when you were 6, probably doesn't work at 30. And what you choose at 60 is likely very different than what you choose at 30. You change, the universe changes. The Third Eye chakra and The Hermit work together to bring you the wisdom to reflect on your current path and choose the right direction for you at this moment in time.

CORRESPONDENCE

- **Astrology:** Virgo. Detailed, service, industrious, efficient
- **Rune:** Iza: Ice. Rune of concentration, stillness
- **I Ching:** Hexagram 36 Ming Yi: Brightness Hiding. When there is adversity, continue to shine your light regardless of what or who confronts you
- **Symbol:** Open Hand
- **Animal:** Hermit crab
- **Element:** Earth

∼

READING CARD PLACEMENT

When The Hermit appears, it means that for now, you should walk alone. Use reflection and solitude to examine your life, where you are, where you wish to go. Step back and evaluate the path you are on. Does it fit your values? Have you changed; does it still work for you? Spend time alone, contemplating what it is you need and desire.

The Hermit is always alone and solitary either by personal choice or imposed on us by outside factors. Whenever the Hermit card appears in a reading, alone time is called for, along with serious reflection and contemplation. Enjoy the solitude and being with your own thoughts. You may need to break with traditions and holds on you to move forward.

Past

You have recently been alone, either to reflect on your life or avoid something. You created a new path in life. The cards in the reading will tell you if the meditation was a positive one that you used to move forward or if you chose to avoid your issues.

Present

When The Hermit appears in the present, it may mean that you are or need to be taking time out as you consider your life, your values, a situation. Use your intuition to guide you. Work through the meanings and options. Use your intuition to find the way through and discover the next steps. Accept their input for analysis, but don't let others influence you to choose a way that is wrong for you.

Future

You can use the wisdom of the Hermit to guide your future. Be prepared for a period of solitude or going it alone. But don't panic. If you accept the Hermit's wisdom, you will move forward on your true path. The insight you gain from following your intuition will benefit you, no matter what area of life you are focusing on.

YES / NO KEY INTERPRETATION

Usually, the Hermit is a no or maybe. The Hermit is telling you to reflect and your inner wisdom will guide you.

KEYWORDS

Solitude, Inner Wisdom, Reflection, Observe, Seek.

11

THE WHEEL OF FORTUNE

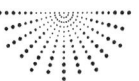

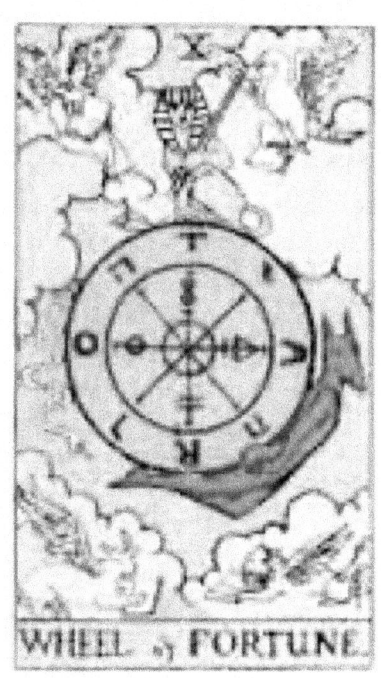

The Wheel of Fortune is a highly symbolic card. It is considered a karma card. Against a background of a blue sky and puffy clouds, it is illustrated with a giant wheel, with three figures on the outer edges, a sphynx, snake, and an Anubis. In the middle of the wheel are four Hebrew letters, YHVH, or Yahweh, the unpronounceable name of God. On the outer circle are the letters TORA, for Torah, meaning 'law'. Some say they could be ROTA, which is Latin for 'wheel'. The middle wheel has the symbols for mercury, sulphur, water, salt, and the four elements.

On top of the wheel sits a Sphinx, representing knowledge. The snake on the left outer edge of the wheel is the Egyptian god Typhon, a god of evil, representing the descent into the material world. On the right side is the Anubis, the Egyptian God of the dead who leads souls to the underworld. On the wheel, they rotate eternally, changing our lives, as do the seasons.

In the corners of the card are four-winged creatures representing the four fixed signs of the Zodiac: Aquarius (angel), Scorpio (eagle), Leo (lion), and Taurus (bull). Each holds the Torah, a sign of wisdom. Their wings signify stability amidst movement and change, and each carries the Torah, representing wisdom. Symbolic of the cycles of life, the Wheel of Fortune is a strong and powerful card. It is an inspiring card because wheels turn and what is at the bottom, comes to the top. Life brings death; death brings life. Knowledge leads us down new paths. The Wheel of Fortune speaks to your destiny and indicates a significant change. Use this time to develop and grow as the universe guides you.

The Wheel of Fortune is about the cycles in the world and your life. Think of the process of birth to death as we go through it. The Wheel, however, also talks about our personal cycles. Consider the familiarity principle. A basic psychology principle it states that humans are attracted to the familiar. Our unconscious will bring the same types of people into our lives because it views them as familiar and therefore safe. On some level we believe we already know how these people will act and react. And how we will respond. It is the unknown that scares us. The Wheel of Fortune reminds us that cycles are normal, but harmful in certain cases. On occasion, we need to break the cycle to find a new way of being in the world.

Generally, the Wheel of Fortune is telling you that good luck is coming your way. There will be positive outcomes. The other cards that surround it will tell you if that luck will be in your finances, love, or career. Regardless of the area, you will be happy. The Wheel of Fortune also symbolizes fate, that which you can't avoid. You are about to receive your destiny. Don't fear this, it is all good. Instead, open your arms to the good luck and change that is about to invade your life.

The Wheel of Fortune can also be named:

- Fortuna
- Destiny
- La Rotta

NUMBER 10 SYMBOLISM

The 10th card in the major arcana, the number 10 signifies completion. A cycle has been completed, the end of a process, the beginning of another. Ten is seen as independent with infinite potential.

When the number 10 appears, look for the opportunities that will come your way. Take advantage of them, and you will become successful. Have faith for destiny is leading you. Explore your options and see what the universe has to offer you.

According to the Pythagoreans, number ten was the holiest of numbers. They took their oaths by number ten. For Pythagoras, 10 was the symbol of the universe and expressed the whole of human knowledge.

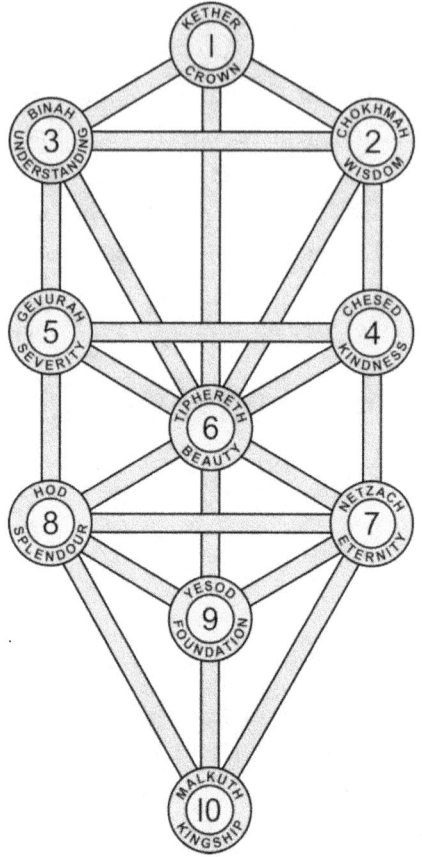

The Wheel of Fortune is on the 21st path in the Tree of Life, called Kapth or palm of the hand. It connects Chesed and Netzach. An open hand invites you into the world. When you open your hand, you are receptive to receiving what the universe has to offer. Your energy is saying that you willingly connect to others and want to work with them. On this path, you can collaborate and create with others. While The Wheel of Fortune contains destiny, this path gives you free will. You can choose the karma of The Wheel of Fortune and use it in a way that fulfills your visions. While fate is pre-determination, what we chose to do with this fate is our free will.

Kapth also creates an energy of creativity and opportunity. On this path, you align your values with your pursuits. Your spiritual goals will meet your physical plans and create great opportunity. You have a new perspective and understand the cycle you are on and where you are placed on The Wheel of Fortune. Kapth allows you choice. Just as The Wheel of Fortune can indicate a harmful cycle, Kapth can close the open hand into a fist. Be aware of who and what you trust. Learn to understand your cycles, and when to extend your open palm. And when to close your hand tight into a fist.

CHAKRA

The Wheel of Fortune corresponds to the Throat chakra. The Throat chakra provides emotional strength and focus with determination, so we can handle the cycles of The Wheel of Fortune. The Throat chakra gives us sound and the vibration of energy throughout our body. This chakra enhances our communication and allows us to express ourselves truthfully. Through this chakra, we can use the Kepth path on the Tree of Life to fine-tune our destiny and move to our future.

The Throat Chakra, called Vishuddha (Pure), is located at the center of the neck. The chakra's symbol has sixteen smoky-purple petals, which represent the sixteen energies associated with the Throat Chakra. This chakra allows you to speak your truth. Through it, you can express yourself, your values, your goals, and your purpose. The throat chakra helps us communicate and project our dreams and visions into the world.

This chakra connects our spirituality to our intuitive abilities. Like

The Wheel of Fortune, the Throat chakra helps you create and move your dreams into reality. If your Throat Chakra is blocked, your ability to handle the cycles of your life will be hampered. Use The Wheel of Fortune's skills to open your Throat chakra, allowing your intuition to come to the forefront once again. If you cannot speak about your visions and goals, then your destiny cannot be fulfilled, for it is only when these are released into the air that the universe perks up and responds to your voice, creating the atmosphere that will lead you to success.

CORRESPONDENCES

- **Astrology:** Leo. Ruling planet is Jupiter
- **Rune:** Pethro: mystery
- **I Ching:** Hexagram 55 Feng: Abundance. When life gifts you, accept the gifts, no matter how small. The abundance may not continue but don't be sad, shine and appreciate what you have in the moment
- **Symbol:** Wheel
- **Animal:** Eagle
- **Element:** Fire

～

Reading Card Placement

The upright Wheel of Fortune indicates that the universe is working to help you reach your goals. Good luck is coming. Your true destiny is coming to you, and you have the opportunity to refine it and make it your own. Your future is fated, but The Wheel of Fortune allows you to adapt it to your values and needs. Remember that life goes in cycles. Things go around and come back to you again.

Past

What you did in your past will dictate how your present and future roll-out. If you were immoral or allowed others to take you down the wrong path, you will have to ride the wheel's cycle to adjust your future to a positive outcome. If you stuck to your values and worked with your destiny, your future is assured to be great.

Present

Changes are coming or are here. Your destiny is set, but you can adjust it to meet your desires if you adhere to your values and reflect on what will truly benefit you. Life can be magical. Smile, for goodness is approaching.

Future

You will be given the opportunity to change your life and develop your goals. You should spend time reflecting and meditating to ensure you are ready. You may need to change your thinking or actions. Regardless, this change will be right for you, making you bright and happy.

YES / NO KEY INTERPRETATION

The answer is yes. The Wheel of Fortune is a positive, enhancing card.

KEYWORDS

Surrender, cycles, fate, wisdom.

12

JUSTICE

Justice sits in front of a purple veil, which signifies wisdom and power, but partially hides the golden light in the sky. Once justice is served, the veil can drop, exposing the full light. The stone seat she sits on is between two grey pillars symbolizing mercy, severity and the law's structure. Justice holds a sword in her right hand and scales in her left.

Some believe that Justice represents Athena, the Greek goddess of war, law, and justice.

The sword points upwards, a sign of logic and order. This is someone who will make fair but firm decisions. Like all swords in the Tarot, this sword is double-edged, reminding you that a blade cuts both ways and that your actions have consequences. Justice holds it upright to show you that she is ready for battle if it is necessary. Choose one way, and the sword swings left; choose the other way, and it swings right. There is no second-guessing. Justice is impartial. She will judge you based on the facts and dispense her judgement with fairness.

The scales, in her left-hand, hold intuition and balance out the sword's logic. Her crown's small square shows her clarity of thought, illustrating that she is a careful thinker and evaluator. Justice wears a red robe with a green mantle. The clasp holding her cloak together is a circle inside a square representing protection and equality. Her white shoe shows beneath her clothing as a reminder of the spiritual consequences of all actions.

Justice brings reason and truth, along with justice. She seeks balance and moderation. When you tip the scales, you are tempting karmic fate. When you are making decisions, Justice challenges you to use your intuition and balance it with logic. If you use the previous Tarot trumps, the Joker through to the Hermit to meditate and reflect on your values and your current path, you will find yourself able to make a definite decision. If you need to change, now is the moment to do so. Justice will aid you in evaluating your life and your actions to ensure you achieve balance. You must be honest with yourself; this is not the time to put on blinders or make yourself feel better by ignoring flaws or bad decisions.

Justice demands the truth from you. What is it that you are doing or not doing that is negatively or positively impacting your life? What can you change to enhance your success? Now is not the time to play the victim. Take control of your life and seek a positive resolution and path to the future. If you have been victimizing others, now is the time to stop and seek forgiveness from those you have harmed. If you don't, Justice will rain her retribution upon you.

Justice is also called:

- Athena
- Daughter of the Lords of Truth
- The Ruler of Balance

NUMBER 11 SYMBOLISM

The number 11 is considered a Master Number because it is a double-digit of the same number. In numerology, this means that it resonates at an unusually high vibration as its energy is double. It is associated with spirituality. Number 1 represents new beginnings and purity, making 11 twice that energy.

Eleven also represents balance in all things: night and day, male and female, physical reality and spiritual reality, sun and moon. Like the Justice card, number 11 wants you to balance your life. It is working with the Justice card to remind you of that balance. Work and play, emotion and logical thought, your feminine side with your masculine side.

JUSTICE | 115

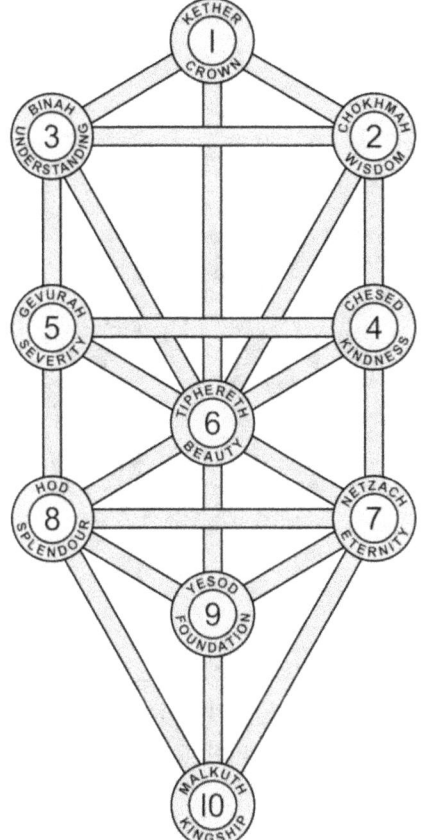

The question asked by the number 11 is 'Are you centered?'. Eleven intuitively knows the answer to this question. A dynamic number, it has a highly developed intuition.

On the Tree of Life, Justice is on the 22nd path, meaning Lamed, or Ox. This path connects Geburah (strength) with Tiphereth (beauty). This path represents balance and adjustment. Combine Justice with the number 11 and this path, and you have a triple influence on balance in your life. On the Lamed path you balance your strength and knowledge with beauty, just as Justice balances logic with intuition.

Lamed is an essential path as it connects to the divine mystery. Only those who have walked this path and experienced the mystery can understand it. When you walk this path, you are acquiring knowledge. The knowledge that will guide you into balance and justice.

When you have learned this knowledge, you will have the skills to lead others in their search for spiritual growth.

CHAKRA

The heart chakra is positioned in the center of your chest, to the right of your heart. In Sanskrit, its name is Anahata (unstuck). It creates your capacity for compassion, openness, affection, and love. Colored green, it is considered the 4th energy center, bridging your earthly desires with the spiritual. It is represented by two triangles forming a 6-pointed star in a circle with 12 petals. The triangles represent the element of air and the union of opposites: male and female, earth and spirit. As Justice does, the heart chakra seeks to open you to your polarities and bring the opposites into harmony and balance.

This chakra works with Justice to bring balance and truth to your life. It can aid you in feeling empathy and compassion for others. It will help you change and move forward in peace. The heart chakra reminds you that truth and justice create a needed balance in life.

The heart chakra is about giving and receiving along with creating balance between the two opposites. Working with Justice, the chakra aims to teach you about truth, honesty, and balance. Justice wants you to face the truth about yourself, to love yourself and love others through that process. Be open to receiving the gift of love from others. This is love from and to all others, not just romantic love.

The heart chakra helps us see the beauty in the world. It is what leaves us awestruck when we stand in front of a fantastic work of art like Botticelli's The Birth of Venus. Or when we stop to admire a beautiful garden instead of just striding on by. Or love a wrinkled, old man looking newborn. We see the beauty, and our hearts blossom.

CORRESPONDENCE

- **Astrology:** Libra. Ruling planet is Venus
- **Rune:** Tiwaz /Tyr, the Sky God. Indicates honor, justice, leadership, authority
- **I Ching:** Hexagram 52 Ken: Stilling. It is time to be quiet, meditative until it is time for movement. Let go of your ego
- **Symbol:** Scales of Justice
- **Animal:** Elephant
- **Elephant:** Air

∽

READING CARD PLACEMENT

Justice is a card of justice and balance. Justice uses her fairness to expose the truth and to make judgements according to the law. When Justice appears in a reading you need to evaluate your actions; past, present and planned actions. You will be judged accordingly.

If you are in alignment with your values, all will go well. If you are out of alignment, correct your path, and own up to your actions. Justice is compassionate when you open up, reveal the truth, and are honest. Take responsibility.

Past

When the Justice card appears in the past position, you are building on the actions you took and the work you performed in the past. Decisions you made will affect the present and possibly the future. Options you made created a new life for you. You had many paths you could have taken, and you made a decision to follow one. The choice could be a good one or a negative one. The outcomes are available to you now.

Present

You have decision to make, and these decisions will impact your future. You will be judged on this decision, so tread carefully. Consider your values, the truth, and use your inner wisdom to choose the correct path. Justice is fair and uses her logic and intuition to evaluate your past and present decisions.

If previous actions caused pain to others, Justice is giving you the chance to change your ways. Your errors can be fixed as long as you take responsibility. If others were unfair to you, Justice's appearance can indicate that you will now be treated fairly.

Future

Judgement will be occurring in the future so take heed now. Revisit your plans. Are you honest with yourself? Are your actions pure in nature? What decisions are you taking that can impact your future outcomes?

YES / NO KEY INTERPRETATION

The answer is yes, if you stick to your values and are totally honest with yourself.

KEYWORDS

Judgement, law, consequences, responsibility.

13

HANGED MAN

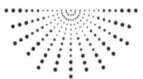

The Hanged Man shows a man suspended from a T-shaped cross made of living wood, a tau cross, often worn by Franciscan friars. Hanging upside-down from a single foot, he views the world from a different perspective. Although used as a punishment in Italy in the middle ages, the Hanged Man is there of his own free will, as shown by the calm expression on his face as he stares back at you. He is bound by his right foot, but his left remains free, bent at the knee and placed behind his other leg, evoking the number 4.

The light that surrounds his head symbolizes enlightenment. His long hair hangs down, partially obscuring the light. The Hanged Man's hands are behind his back, forming an inverted triangle. We don't know if they are tied there or if he is deliberately holding them that way on his own. He is wearing red pants to show his passion and a blue shirt that reflects his serenity and growing knowledge. The tree is rooted deep in the earth and reaches up to the heavens.

The Hanged Man is a card of surrender and of suspension in time. It is a symbol of meditation, selflessness, and trial. The universe is suggesting to you that it is a time of surrender. Not in the negative sense of losing something, but in a positive way; surrendering to your destiny and allowing the universe to take over.

Having inverted himself, The Hanged Man knows that he must stay still and reflect on his next actions. Subject to gravity, he is being pulled to the earth, but his foot, firmly tied, holds him to the heavens. The yellow light around his head glows with his spirit and new knowledge. Soon he will release himself from this position, but for now, he is content to hang and learn.

A card of sacrifice, The Hanged Man tells you that sometimes you must give up something to gain. You must do so from a place of power and surrender, not from a position of martyrdom or victimhood. For newness to arrive in your life, you must make space for it by releasing something in your life that has outlived its time. This may be something that is easy to let go of, or it may cause you sadness and grief. Even when you know it is time to release, you can still feel a deep regret for what you are losing.

Remember, that like The Hanged Man, you are choosing to surrender, choosing to sacrifice so that you can move forward, using the light that surrounds The Hanged Man's head. The outcome is uncertain but relax while you wait. Gather all the information you need before proceeding. The Hanged Man tells you that action is not what is required. Meditation, calmness and belief will work to enhance your life and the lives of those around you.

Another name for The Hanged Man is:

- Norse god Odin
- El Cogado
- Le Pendu

NUMBER 12 SYMBOLISM

Number 12 in the Major Arcana, The Hanged Man's card number is considered the perfect number. Twelve is the number of completion and of the whole. Twelve symbolizes good and creativity. In some religions, it is a sign of the Divine Mother. This belief stems from the fact that 12 represents the creation of the universe.

Twelve appears everywhere in Western society and in Christian-Judeo culture. There are 12 tribes of Israel, 12 Apostles, and 12 members of a jury. Time is based on the number 12. There were 12 Greek gods. Odin, the Norse god, had 12 sons. There are 12 months in a year.

The number 12 represents a full circle, harmony, and order. The Hanged Man is searching for that order and desires unity. It gives you a bowl of plenty. With 12, you have reached a whole.

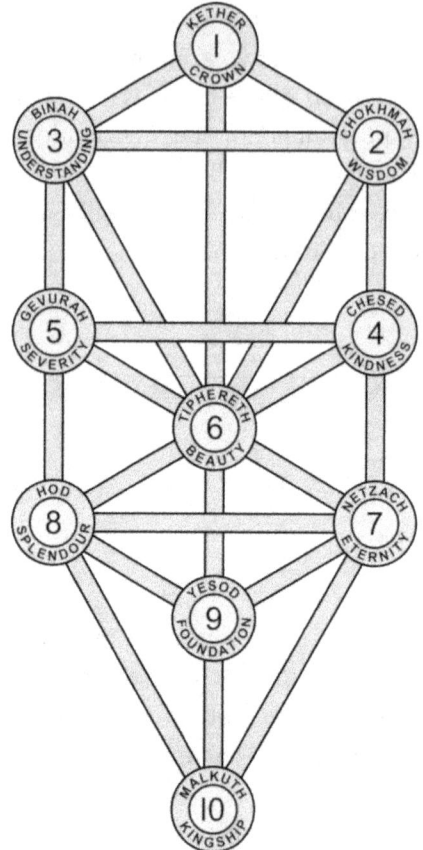

On the Tree of Life, The Hanged Man sits on the 12th path, between Geburah (instability) and Hod (knowledge). Called Mem in Hebrew, meaning Water or Spirit of the Mighty Water. Human beings are composed mainly of water, and likewise our planet. Without water, life is unsustainable. Water finds its way. If you've ever had a flood or a roof leak, you will know that water seeps everywhere, going around anything that it is in its way. And like rocks in a stream, water wears down what it consistently flows over.

Mem is related to creation. This is a place of quiet contemplation, dealing with emotions. Life is at standstill and you must sit and contemplate before you can move forward. Use the Hanged Man to mediate and gain understanding where you need to go next.

CHAKRA

The Crown chakra is the chakra of Divine Oneness and symbolized by the thousand-petalled lotus. This chakra represents pure consciousness or bliss. An energy center that functions at its best when we let go of our ego's need to be in charge.

Known as Sahasrara in Sanskrit, the crown chakra is the seventh chakra. Located on the crown of the head, it is associated with spirituality. The Sahasrara chakra is violet or white, represented by a lotus flower with a thousand petals. This chakra allows people to move from materialism to the wholeness of spirituality. Opening the crown chakra brings insight and confidence to your life.

The Root chakra grounds us on the Earth, while the Crown chakra's energy connects us to the universal whole and the creation of newness. With this chakra, you experience oneness and a feeling that everything is related at the source. Your crown chakra emanates a peaceful and calm feeling.

The Hanged Man is seeking this chakra's wisdom. He has encountered challenges that leave him confused, so he is surrendering and waiting patiently for the knowledge to guide him forward.

CORRESPONDENCES

- **Astrology:** Pisces.
- **Rune:** Eihwaz / Yew Tree
- **I Ching:** Hexagram 49 Ko: Revolution. A revolution in your life begins. Life is cyclical and success is noted for you
- **Symbol:** Tau Cross
- **Animal:** Peacock
- **Element:** Water

∼

READING CARD PLACEMENT

When The Hanged Man appears in a reading, it often means that things are not moving forward in your life. You are standing still, either self-imposed or by other's actions. You may be feeling frustrated or stuck, out of control. But this is your opportunity to pause and take stock of your situation. A time out is called for so you can gather input and knowledge before taking action. There may be sacrifices.

Past

The Hanged Man in the past position tells you that your present situation began by you letting go and retreating. You gave up something in order to get where you are today. You made a decision to let go of something or someone and move forward.

Present

You are in a situation where a sacrifice is required before you can move forward. The Hanged Man is telling you to stop and contemplate. What is it that you are missing? What should you leave behind as you strive towards future goals? Surrender to the moment, curb your impatience and wait. This is not the time to action. It is the time to rethink what you are doing and what you need to continue.

Future

A time is coming where you will need to stop and reflect on your actions. The card in your present place will indicate what you are working on that may need adjustment. A relationship, a career, a move, travel. When this arrives, greet it with calmness and take the offer to surrender into meditation.

YES / NO KEY INTERPRETATION

The answer is No for the moment. Let go.

KEYWORDS

Sacrifice, Release, Letting go, Surrender.

14

DEATH

Death, card 13, brings beginnings and endings, change, and sudden turmoil. The Death card shows the Messenger of Death riding a white horse. He is a skeleton dressed in black armor and carrying a banner with the mystic rose, a white, five petal-rose; a symbol of life and purity on it.

We cannot avoid death; it is the inevitable end that comes to all of us. On the right-hand side, a fiery setting sun illustrating immortality sets between two pillars.

A person lays dead on the ground, while others cry out to be spared. A king, a peasant, male, female, all races, Death doesn't care; he will reach all. Death comes to us all, but those still alive want to avoid it as long as possible. Death arrives as a skeleton on a battlefield, littered with bones, limbs, and heads. If you look closely, you see plants growing from the battlefield's wreckage, reminding us of the cycle of life. Endings may come, but spring and new births will arrive.

The Tarot Death card represents endings and beginnings. It is not a card that predicts an actual death but rather is about change, often drastic and transformational. It tells you that things will change in your life, and like death, change is inevitable. There is an old saying, 'If you haven't changed in the last 5 years, check your pulse. You may be dead'.

To avoid change is to avoid life. You can be stuck in a soulless existence if you resist changes in your life. The Death card is a powerful and positive card. For with each change comes renewal, opportunities, and rejuvenation of life. A significant part of your life has finished, and it is time to let it go and welcome the new and exciting prospects that will appear. Get ready to grasp new opportunities that are coming to you.

This is your opportunity to bring change and advancements into your life. This could be about a relationship, your behaviors, a career opportunity, the birth of a child or any other numerous opportunities and life enhancers. This change may come as a shock but release your knee-jerk reactions and embrace it. This change is significant and can't be avoided. Be open to it, even if it looks scary and uninviting. Hold your judgement and wait to see how it improves your life. Letting go can be difficult, but acceptance is necessary. Be joyful and forward-looking as you evaluate this change and its impact on your life.

The Death card is also known as:

- Messenger of Death
- The Card with No Name
- Grim Reaper

NUMBER 13 SYMBOLISM

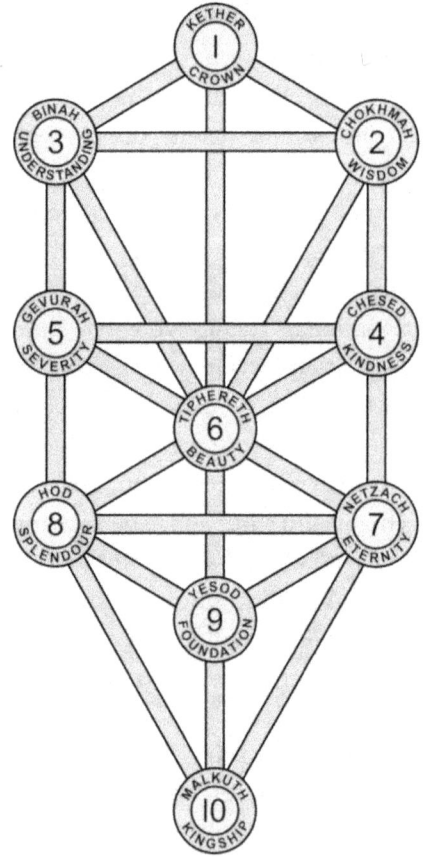

Death is the 13th card in the major arcana. The number 13 is often considered unlucky by those who are superstitious, believing it to be an unfortunate number that results in terrible things happening. Hotels will 'omit' floor 13, jumping from 12 to the 14th floor.

But in fact, there are equally as many who believe the number is powerful and lucky. The Aztecs considered thirteen a sacred number that represented completion. An Aztec week lasted for thirteen days. Ancient Egyptians also considered it an auspicious number. Some Christians believe that 13 is the number of the Virgin Mary. (This contrasts with the story of Last Supper, where 13 disciples attended.) In ancient Greek mythology, the god Zeus, powerful and capable, was numbered 13.

As the mythology surrounding the number flips between 2 opposites, so the number 13 purifies and cleans, much as Death does. It throws away your past and lets in your future. It symbolizes the death of the old ways and brings you into a higher spiritual plane. For some Christians, the number 13 is a sign of the Virgin Mary. For others, it is an evil number, probably originating from the fact that there were 13 people at the last supper; Jesus and 12 disciples. Judas is considered the 13th apostle, and he is the one who betrays Jesus.

Death is on the 13th pathway of the Tree of Life. The Hebrew name of this path is Nun, which means Fish. Nun is the path of depth and intimacy, think of swimming in dark water. Just like the card Death, it indicates transformation and renewal. When you travel Nun, you move from Tiphereth (beauty) to Netzach (victory). The Death card moves you to victory as well, even though your initial reaction to the change may be adverse or skeptical.

Death releases you from this physical world into the spiritual world. You become reborn. This path asks you to re-evaluate and trust your intuition. Logic will not help you at the moment. It is time to use your intuition and dive into your unconscious.

CHAKRA

The Crown chakra is the chakra of Divine Oneness and is known as the 'thousand-petalled lotus.' It is pure consciousness and bliss. This energy center functions fully when we let go of our egos and allow others to be in control, be right, and walk their own paths without criticizing them.

The crown chakra, called Sahasrara in Sanskrit, is the 7th chakra, located on the crown of the head. Associated with spirituality, the Sahasrara chakra is violet and white, represented by a lotus flower with a thousand petals. This chakra moves people from materialism to connect with the greater universe. Opening the crown chakra brings spiritual insight, mindfulness, and the ability to live with quiet self-confidence in all aspects of life.

The gift of this chakra is to experience unity while understanding that everything is connected on all levels. The Crown chakra's energy guides us to the mystical oneness with everyone and everything in nature. In many ways, it represents the Jungian theory of the collective consciousness. Jung's theory posits that part of our unconscious mind is genetically inherited and common to all human beings. Commonly held beliefs and instincts are shared by us all through the collective unconscious, similar to how the Crown chakra brings us oneness.

This understanding is not logical, nor is there any intellectual thought process attached to the 7th chakra. This is a more profound knowledge, that happens on a spiritual level, intuitive level, and produces a sense of joy and peace. You begin understanding the deeper meaning of life and connecting with others in a new way. This chakra, like Death, is about ending, letting go of the physical world, emerging into the light of the spirit.

CORRESPONDENCES

- **Astrology:** Scorpio
- **Rune:** Ansuz: insight, harmony and wisdom
- **I Ching:** Hexagram 12 P'i Stagnation, Obstruction. A time of loss. Things around you are at a standstill. Use your inner strength to get through
- **Symbol:** Pentagram
- **Animal:** Goat
- **Element:** Water

READING CARD PLACEMENT

The Death card signals that a significant stage of your life is ending, leaving space for a new phase to start. Let go, put the past behind you and use your energy to take advantage of the new opportunities. Break with the past.

Past

You experienced a change in your life, moving you from one aspect to another. This may have been painful, but it was necessary, and now you are moving forward into the new.

Present

You are in the midst of change and transformation. You may feel unsure as you move into the new space but accept and welcome the change. Open the door to the newness that is coming. Let go of unhealthy attachments and habits. Letting go and moving forward is healthy and invigorating, and the Death card teaches us this.

Future

Drastic change is coming. Prepare yourself to embrace the change and find lightness in the new energy coming your way. You cannot avoid this change, so move forward and learn from it. A relationship may end (marriage, job, or another aspect of your life).

YES / NO KEY INTERPRETATION

The Death card indicates dramatic change and a new beginning. Work through the changes and ask again. The answer is no.

KEYWORDS

Change, endings, new beginnings, transformation.

15

TEMPERANCE

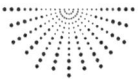

Temperance comes from the Latin teperare, meaning to blend together. Temperance is one of Plato's 4 cardinal values and adopted by Christian theologists: Prudence, Courage, Justice, and Temperance.

A large angel adorns the Temperance card. Some people believe the angel to be the angel Gabriel. Wings spread, it wears a light white robe with the yellow sun reflecting off it and a triangle on the front, suggesting her connection to the holy trinity and to balance. Angels are not considered to be of either gender but often referred to with the she pronoun. They balance both masculine and feminine energy. The angel has one foot placed on the shore, keeping her grounded to the earth. The other foot, dips into the water, where she feels unconscious emotions, reminding you that your intuition is invaluable, and you must listen to and trust it.

The angel pours water between 2 cups, illustrating the flow between the unconscious and the conscious mind, reminding us to blend and merge them. The cups she uses represent creativity and how we use both logic and intuition to create our visions. The card symbolizes union, balance, harmony, and the merging of opposites.

Her red and black wings symbolize power. This power is brought to her by her ability to blend and find balance in all. The wings are large, and she must be strong to manage them as she flies, especially as life will throw strong winds at her. Behind her is a path that winds up a mountain; this is your life journey, a long twisting way but full of beauty along with the obstacles. Above the mountains the sun shines, a sign of light and spirit that you walk towards. If you stay true to yourself, to your values, you are blessed with this light. This card is a peaceful image, full of beauty.

Two yellow flowers bloom, showing you the beauty that naturally occurs when you blend your unconscious thoughts with your conscious logic. The angel's head is surrounded by light as she mixes the water in her cups. Inside her, despite any external turmoil, the angel maintains her balance and harmony. Through this harmony, she has developed a strong sense of who she is, and this sense of self guides her through life, allowing her to maintain her separateness and observe others and situations with calm. She involves herself in life but only through her solid foundation of self.

When you can step back and clearly assess your own inner values, you can deal with the chaos of life and keep yourself firmly on your path to the light. Self-knowledge enhances your relationships with others and expands your life force.

The Temperance Major Arcana card is also known as:

- Fferyllt (Gaelic)
- La Temperanza
- Art
- Time

NUMBER 14 SYMBOLISM

Temperance is the 14th Major Arcana card. Number 14 is symbolic of Sagittarius and associated with balance. Fourteen asks you to have patience and wait for knowledge. 14 grounds you, bringing reality to your dreams.

In Christianity, number 14 is considered spiritual, representing salvation. In numerology, the number 14 represents self-determination, a trait that Temperance brings to us by self-awareness gained through balance. As Temperance guides us to creativity and balance, number 14 gives us the ability to produce while ignoring others' doubts. Fourteen encourages us to be curious and interested in the world.

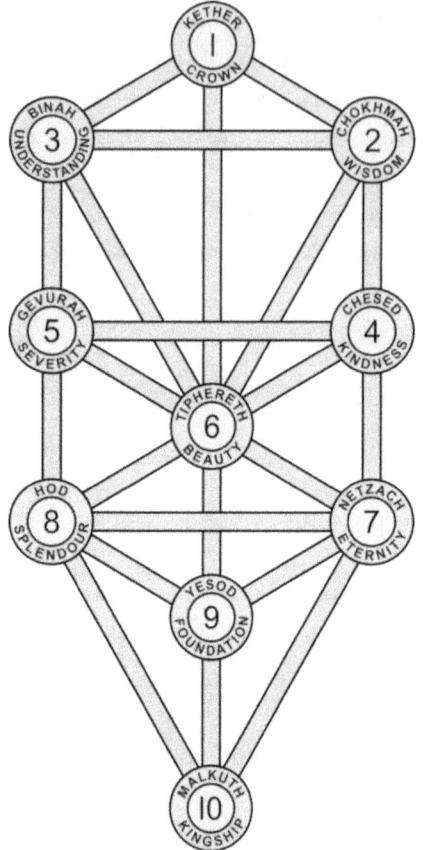

It is thought that 14 expresses freedom, self-determination, and curiosity. Number 14 gives you the focus and interest to develop your dreams into reality. The moon waxes and wanes for 14 days each month. Currently, the Dalai Lama is in his 14th incarnation. Makar Sankranti festival is considered a day of good fortune and is celebrated throughout India on the 14th of January.

In the tree of life, Temperance correlates with the 25th path, Samekh meaning staff. Samekh connects Yesod (foundation) with Tiphereth (beauty). This path represents balance, strength, and alignment. When Samekh appears in the form of the Temperance Tarot card, you are on a path to enlightenment and developing your spirituality.

Samekh is symbolized by an arrow being shot straight into the air, hence the astrological association of Temperance to Sagittarius. The path of Samekh brings you to light and awareness. With the Samekh path, you are evolving into a mature being who can balance their emotions and thoughts, actions, and stillness. Just as Temperance asks, you are reaching for your higher self. This is a difficult path, as balance and self-awareness don't come easily. You may stumble around in darkness before you emerge into the light. You are harmonizing yourself, finding that perfect blend from which your true self will emerge. Remember that little is black and white, most of what we encounter in life is grey, and your job is to find the balance between 2 opposites.

CHAKRA

According to Hindu tradition, Anahata or heart chakra is the fourth primary chakra. In Sanskrit, Anahata means unhurt, unstruck, and unbeaten.

Anahata helps you move love through your life by creating bonds with other people and increasing your compassion and caring. The heart chakra opens your eyes to assist you in viewing people in a positive light and respect them for their goodness, despite their flaws. Anahata brings wholeness to your life. It is considered your healing center, where you can heal yourself and others.

Located in the center of your chest, it is the 4th chakra and reflects the color green. It is symbolized by a green 6-pointed star in a circle with 12 petals. The heart chakra helps us love ourselves and others, involves us in relationships, and through those relationships, generates acceptance and growth. We change as we allow ourselves to experience empathy and gather insights through these relationships.

The energy of Anahata allows us to recognize that we are part of something larger, that we are interconnected within an intricate web of relationships extending through life and the universe. The Heart Chakra allows us to know the sacred truth. It embodies love for oneself and for others. The Heart Chakra has the ability to transform and change us using awareness and insight.

Anahata allows us to recognize and get in touch with the sacred and fundamental truth that runs through all of life and connects everything together. When you live your life with this energy, you vibrate with love.

CORRESPONDENCE

- **Astrology:** Sagittarius. Adjustment, creating balance and constructive activity
- **Rune:** Doges: dawn, clarity, light, a positive change
- **I Ching:** Hexagram 57 Sun. Gentle Penetration. Gentle success. It comes in small waves not a large bang. Be a good influence
- **Symbol:** Golden cup
- **Animal:** Heron, Swan
- **Element:** Fire

~

READING CARD PLACEMENT

Temperance brings balance, patience, and moderation into your life. It is time for you to balance your energy and thoughts. Bring calmness to any appearing issues. Use this balance to create order out of chaos. Temperance is a powerful card. When you are balanced, your creativity will blossom. Use your intuition.

Past

You remained calm, despite issues and concerns in your life. This helped you grow and become more balanced and thus, truer to yourself. This is a great place from which to take on the present and future.

Present

Breath deep and access your unconscious. Blend your reality with your intuition to find the way forward. Use your values to create balance. Spend some time meditating to connect with your spiritual side. Find a quiet place and listen to your inner voice. If you start a project now, you will be successful. You feel peaceful and self-assured. Use this time of peace to be creative.

Future

Start now to plan for the future by seeking balance. Be true to yourself and use your self-assurance to find the way forward. You will experience a burst of creativity and can start new projects with confidence. Use the present to prepare for this phase.

YES / NO KEY INTERPRETATION

The answer is yes, as long as you are balanced and harmonized with your true self.

KEYWORDS

Guidance, peace, balance, contentment, home, freedom, curiosity, self-determination.

16
THE DEVIL

Card number 15 in the Major Arcana is The Devil. Known by many names (Baphomet, Goat god), The Devil card is a difficult card to receive in a reading unless it is in your past or tempered with other cards.

The Devil card shows a satyr, a half-goat, half-man mythical form. He has large bat wings, an inverted pentagram on his forehead, horns of a ram, and is obese from his gluttony. His hairy animal legs end in bird talons, which grip the altar he is sitting on. According to Waite, the altar is only half an altar because 'the Devil only knows half the world.' He knows the debased, materialistic, tormented side of reality. This inability to understand himself renders The Devil incapable of making clear, positive, life-enhancing decisions. He is chained by his own limited knowledge.

The card background is black. The Devil raises one hand and lowers the other with a lit torch illustrating his control. The Devil pulls the chains of the nude man and woman who are chained to the altar. The chains hang loosely around their necks. If they choose, they could lift the chains off and walk away, releasing themselves from their own self-inflicted bondage. Both have horns and tails, illustrating that the longer they stay with the Devil, the more they transform into him and take on his values. Looking at their tails, you see they are bound to the Devil through addiction to power and lust (fire) along with pleasure in materialism and gluttony (grapes). They are allowing their past choices in life to dictate their future. Unless they release themselves from bondage, they will continue to have a difficult time in life – bad relationships, careers or work they dislike, and issues with family members.

What is interesting is that the couple is not happy in this bondage. The man and woman feel exposed and ashamed, but The Devil won't voluntarily let them go; they must lift the chains on their own. The bat wings of The Devil tell you that he will suck your lifeblood, leaving you empty. Once you give into your raw desires, without considering your values and correct path in life, The Devil takes over, hypnotizing you and using his darkness to keep you enslaved. When you choose the path of The Devil, you are choosing instant gratification, without regard to your long-term goals and values. This leaves you feeling out of control, that others or circumstances are running your life.

To move forward into a positive life, you need to acknowledge that The Devil has you in his grip and is causing problems and issues in your life. Whatever your conditions, whatever you believe or think, you can take action to release yourself. Look deeply at what you have been doing, at what has caught you. Understand that materialism will not fill your soul. It often leaves you feeling emptier than you felt before you obtained that luxury. Nor will lust or gluttony fill the emptiness.

The Devil has many names including:

- Baphomet
- Horned Goat of Mendes
- Goat-god Dionysius
- Satan
- Mephistopheles
- Luther

NUMBER 15 SYMBOLISM

The Devil's card number 15 refers to the material and spiritual. Indicating the need for balance between your worldly desires and your spiritual growth, number 15 speaks of the flow of energy and our source of power. It represents the duality that plays between our unconscious and our conscious thoughts. The number is curious and easily distracted by other interests (shiny objects). It can lose focus before returning to the right place.

In Christianity, 15 describes the association between the Old Testament and the New Testament as the sum of 7, the Sabbath (Old Testament) and 8, the Resurrection (New Testament). Some claim 15 is the number of Satan (The Devil). On the other hand, there are 15 decade of prayers in the Rosary of the Virgin Mary. Her assumption is celebrated on August 15th.

The Devil is on the 16th path on the tree of life, Ayin, a way to balance between your instinctual base side and your spiritual side. Ayin's symbol is "Y," representing the 2 forces of light and darkness. When you move to wholeness through knowledge and intuition, you can combine those two, creating balance in your life. Ayin connects Tiphereth (beauty) and Hod (splendor). This is a path of earthly matters. Like The Devil, 15 can be pulled to baseness. It gives you a choice between being chained to The Devil or freedom through choosing the balance of the 2nd path.

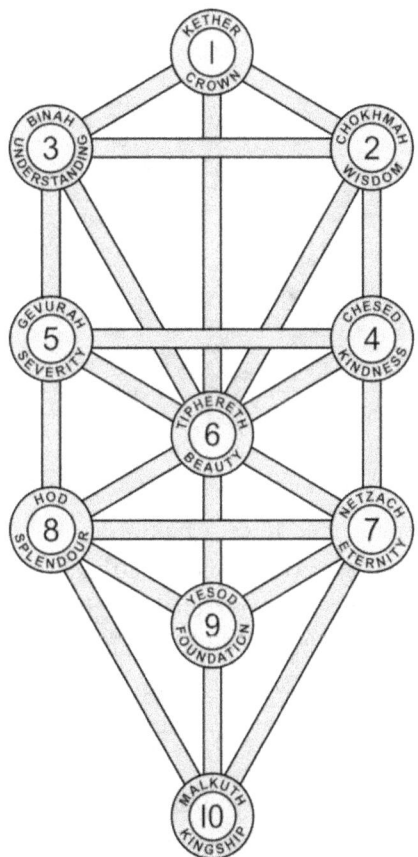

The Devil is an illusion. He can't really control us. It is we who bind ourselves to him and his values. We willingly enslave ourselves to him, putting the chains around our own neck. Instead of seeking balance, we indulge in our dark side by aligning to The Devil. We can use Ayin to free us from those impulses and move to the light side where we are happier and in harmony with our values.

On the Ayin path, we will experience all parts of ourselves. The good, the bad, our shadow side, our light, and blessed side. Just like the couple chained to The Devil, we can lift the chains from our necks and grow in spirit and knowledge.

CHAKRA

An earth element, the Root Chakra, is the first chakra. The Sanskrit name for the root chakra is Muladhara, symbolized by a red lotus with four petals. The root chakra gives you the feeling of safety and a sense of being grounded. Situated at the base of the spine, it lays the foundation for expansion in your life. The first chakra is associated with security, your basic needs and keeps you grounded.

The Root Chakra brings you stability. It is stability that allows you to defeat The Devil. But it is also instinctual. You don't need to think about this chakra; it is part of who you are as a human being, primal in nature. The Root Chakra rules your physical needs such as food, water, and shelter. Think of Maslov's hierarchy of needs. You can't function well in life unless these basic needs are first met. This instinct also warns us of danger, both physical and psychological. Red is a warning color, and The Root Chakra instinctively kicks in when it feels we are encountering difficulties. Red is also the color of The Devil in many images.

The root chakra, when balanced, creates the foundation of security. It is the foundation on which we build our life and allows us to feel safe as we explore our universe. The root chakra gives us wisdom that we can use to release ourselves from The Devil's chains. It provides your ability to trust while you are out in the world. And it aids you in finding your way through the dark into the light.

This chakra oversees your sexuality and the urge to procreate. When the Root Chakra is balanced, the energy flows, and you feel secure and trusting. We can then emerge from The Devil's way and plan for our goals and dreams.

CORRESPONDENCE

- **Astrology:** Capricorn. Ruling planet is Saturn
- **Rune:** Nauthiz: Delays, restriction. Resistance leading to strength, innovation, self-reliance
- **I Ching:** Hexagram 12 P'i. Stagnation, Obstruction. A time of loss. Things around you are at a standstill. Use your inner strength to get through
- **Symbol:** Pentagram
- **Animal:** Goat
- **Element:** Earth

READING CARD PLACEMENT

In Jungian terms, The Devil represents your shadow side. He appears to remind you of the dark pieces of you that constrain you and move you away from your values. If you play with The Devil, you risk losing all. Your life will become fraught with difficulties as you reach for things that in the illusion that they will save you; addictions, materialism, lust for materialism, bad habits, nastiness to others. You may think The Devil traps you, but you trap yourself.

Past

When The Devil card appears in the past position, your dealings with a domineering person or situation are over. At the foundation of your life sits the experience of this intense relationship at its core. But you have new structures in your life from which to operate and excel. It is good news to have The Devil in the past position. The chains have been broken. Your bondage is disappearing.

Present

The Devil appears to warn you of something wrong in your life. Carefully examine all and reflect on your values. Are your relationships with others based on honesty and aligned with your values? Are you in trouble with alcohol or drugs? Is work functioning as it should, shining with honesty, something that produces real value to the world? Consider your material desires and ensure they are not out of line and subsuming other areas of life. For example, are you working long hours for money and neglecting the relationships in your life? Remember, the Devil is not holding you in your bondage. You keep yourself there. Find a way to release yourself.

Future

When The Devil is placed in the future, it is a warning and giving you the opportunity to change. You may attract the wrong kind of people into your life or work towards a goal that doesn't fit with your values. Take the time to do some self-reflection and ensure you self-correct. We all deviate from the correct path; the wise person heeds warnings and steers themselves back to the way that brings balance and harmony.

YES / NO KEY INTERPRETATION

The answer is no. You have work (values realignment, spirituality, psychological) to do to achieve a yes answer.

KEYWORDS

Excess, Greed, Temptation, Unhealthy relationships, Enslavement, Materialism, Bondage, Fear, Feeling trapped.

17

THE TOWER

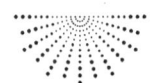

A large tower sits on top of a mountain. Lightning is striking it, causing people to leap from the windows. A crown at the top of the tower is falling. Significant pain, disruption, and change are happening. Flames are emerging from the windows making the people desperate to escape.

The Tower is firm, but it can be quickly brought down because it is built on a bad foundation. This shows how even the best goals or plans, when designed on the wrong foundation, with a lack of logic or checking in with your gut, are doomed to failure.

When confronted with the turmoil and chaos of The Tower, the natural instinct is to want to escape. But remember, The Tower is built on wrong ideas and premises. To move forward, it must be destroyed, so you can bring in the new and correct goals.

The Tower brings destruction. Your beliefs and values are shattered, and the universe is challenging you to change. Everything is falling apart. These events will often be life changing. A marriage or relationship may end, you may lose your job or discover that a way of being you've believed in for years is now exposed as a fraud.

These changes often occur without any warning to you. You may feel as if you have been punched in the gut. Your universe collapses, and you will be forced to change. This is not a time when you get to choose. The world around you is choosing it for you. This destruction may be due to some action that you previously took. Previously, you choose a path that has led you to this moment.

You are being reminded that every decision you make has a consequence. It may take years for you to see the fully evolved outcome, but you will be impacted. If you have chosen wisely, the impact will be positive. If you rushed the decision or choose something that went against your fundamental values, the effect will be negative.

Remind yourself that change, even drastic change, doesn't have to be bad in the long run. The Tower could be opening new doors for you, creating better opportunities, and you will look back in wonder that you thought it was a disaster. And if you open your heart and mind, you will learn that change can be positive. The Tower brings you lessons. If you absorb those lessons now, you will not have to repeat them in the future.

The Tower doesn't want to harm you. It wants to wake you up to full consciousness and create an awareness of what truly matters in your life.

The Tower is also called:

- La Foudre
- The Blasted Tower
- The Fall

NUMBER 16 SYMBOLISM

The Tower is the 16th card in the major arcana. Number 16 is about introspection and reflection. Consider what you have built and why you chose this path. What did you miss along the way? Where did you go wrong? What positive steps did you take that you can now use as you go through this change? Seek a mentor, talk to an old crone, or a wise man to gain wisdom and insight as you move through this change.

On the Tree of Life, The Tower is placed on the 27th path called Peh or Mouth, connecting Hod and Netzach. This is a path of cleansing. It removes behaviors that are no longer appropriate for you. It clears out what isn't working and, like the Phoenix, creates newness from the ashes of destruction.

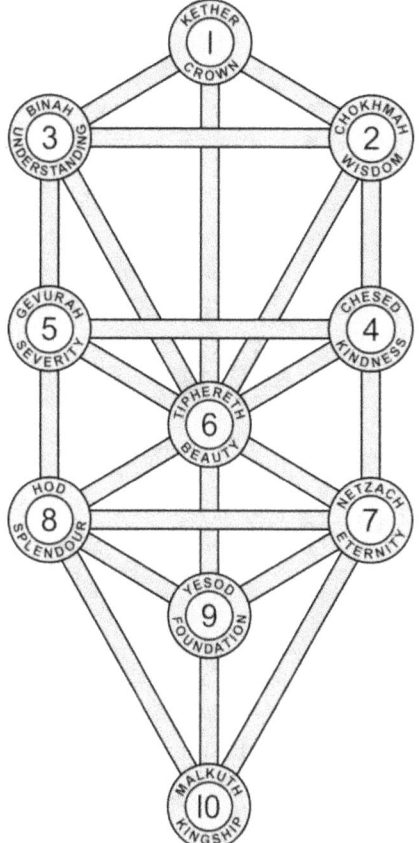

This path is calling on you to let go of your falseness, the facade you face the world with, and let the blinders fall from your eyes. Face your new reality with courage.

The 27th path is also about learning how to express yourself in a way that benefits you and those with whom you interact. If you communicate without thinking or without heart, you risk creating arguments and anger. This path helps you release your ego. It allows you to cool your emotions and use your logic, along with your heart, to temper your speech.

The previous card in the major arcana, The Devil, speaks about moving from your materialistic nature to a spiritual balance. The Tower continues that work. Materialism doesn't fill the soul, and ultimately, The Tower destroys that which is built on it. If your identity is built on materialism, there is no depth, just an emptiness. You must learn to find your true self, your spiritual essence, and cast aside your need for materialism.

CHAKRA

The Tower is associated with the third chakra, the Solar Plexus Chakra, Manipura, meaning shining gem. Located in the solar plexus area, near your diaphragm, it is the 3rd chakra from the bottom. It is illustrated by a golden yellow circle with 10 petals. In the middle is a triangle pointing down. This chakra is also associated with The Chariot, a card that deals with your willpower and sense of purpose in the world. So too, The Tower is changing you, asking you to look again at your values and your goals in the world.

The Solar Plexus chakra, like The Tower, works with our ego. Using this chakra, you can move into action and meet your challenges to move forward. And like The Tower and many other Tarot cards, the chakra requires balance. Balance in using your power, your emotions, and in dealing with the people around you. Power doesn't mean power over others; it means your ability to control your thoughts and feelings and use them in positive life-enhancing ways.

Your solar plexus chakra is working whenever you exert self-control. When The Tower's energy strikes you, use this energy to gain courage. If you are fearful of a situation, adopt a healthy posture; head held high, shoulders back, deep breaths. You will activate the solar plexus chakra, and it will assist you in your challenge.

The solar plexus chakra aids you in following your true path and remember your values. It also helps you have an awareness of the world around you and guard against those things that can pull you away from your values and beliefs. Your ability to achieve your goals is held in the solar plexus chakra.

CORRESPONDENCES

- **Astrology:** Taurus. Ruling planet is Mars
- **Rune:** Hagalaz: Hail, delay and limitations
- **I Ching:** Hexagram 59 Dispersion. Disperse your energy. Cooperate with others and seek out those who have high goals. Check your values and let go of rigid beliefs
- **Symbol:** A Crown
- **Animal:** Vulture, sometimes a lion or a snake
- **Element:** Fire

∽

READING CARD PLACEMENT

The Tower is about shifting energies. It can foretell a change in old ways and values. The falling of The Tower in your life may be unexpected, causing you distress. But ultimately, the goal of The Tower is to bring newness to your life.

Past

The old ways were destroyed to make room for your present life and ambitions. It was difficult and challenging, but you held up and created a future.

Present

Momentous change is happening in your life. This may be unnerving and yet groundbreaking. It may not be a disaster or a terrible event. It can be a large shift in your values, a conflict coming to a head, or other change in your life. Let go of what you've built. It no longer serves you and must be destroyed.

Future

Challenges are coming, but if you prepare, you will find the strength to deal with them and build a brighter future. Check your foundations, values, and beliefs. Are you standing on shaky ground? Start now to invoke changes that will produce a solid base for you.

YES / NO KEY INTERPRETATION

The answer is no. The Tower brings destruction, chaos and major change. Stop and consider the conditions surrounding your question.

KEYWORDS

Sudden change, surrender, beyond your control, quarrels, disruption, upheaval, chaos, awakening.

18

THE STAR

The Star card shows a nude woman with soft golden hair, kneeling at the edge of a small pool, holding two containers, under a night sky. She pours water out of both, with the left hand representing the unconscious and the right the conscious. She waters the earth, with her left hand, the water streaming everywhere, giving rise to fertility and growth, keeping the ground lush and green. With her right hand, she pours water into the pond, creating concentric circles that represent spiritual energy. One foot is dipped in the water showing her spirituality, intuition, and control of her emotions. The other foot is grounded as she kneels, giving her foundation and strength. The woman is naked, exposed, and open to the world with nothing to hide. She is vulnerable and pure at the same time.

Above the woman, a large star shines, with seven smaller ones, surrounding it, representing the seven main chakras. Each star, large and small, has eight points. An Ibis stands in a tree branch representing birth and new beginnings. The eight-pointed star first appeared in Islamic art in the Middle Ages. It is referred to as 'khatim or khatim-sulayman', which means 'seal of the prophets.' The Chinese see the eight-pointed star as a depiction of the universe.

The Star shines a light on you and aids in the renewal of the spirit. It is a positive sign and helps you when you are in need of recovery. The Star gives you the calmness and harmony required to fully recover and move forward. This is not a short-term peace; this calmness will stay for a time giving you hope and renewal. It is a card of reward, for The Star has seen your struggles and is blessing you.

This card is also about creating positive energy. When you give out positive energy to the world, it is returned back to you in abundance. And seeing this energy in the starlight creates a soft vibration, a sense of ease and magic. From this comes hope, regeneration that allows us to create, to love, and to move forward.

Another aspect of The Star is spirituality. The landscape that surrounds the woman speaks of fertility and renewal. It is land that brings spring shoots and, with it, joy. There is a feeling of relaxation coming from the card. It is time to renew yourself, both physically and spiritually, before you start your journey again. The Star asks you to let go of your past and sink into the earth with relief as the stars shine above you.

The Star shines with other names:

- Stella
- The Daughter of the Firmament
- Dweller between the Waters

NUMBER 17 SYMBOLISM

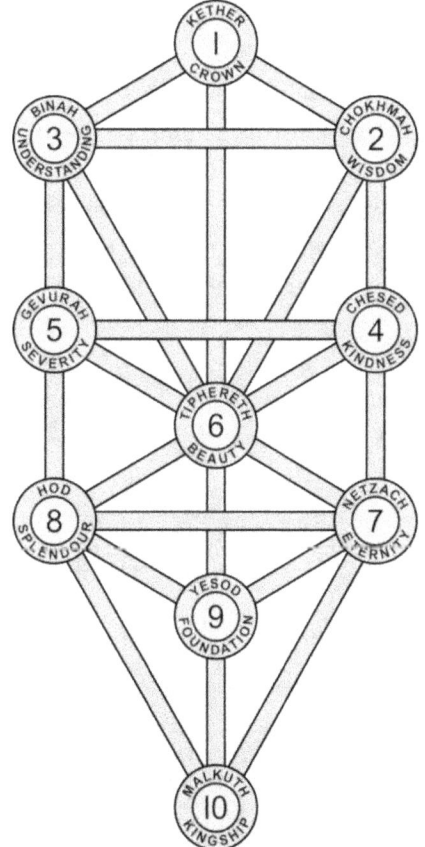

The Star card is number 17 in the Major Arcana. Number 17 is considered to be a happy number with good strong vibrations. As the Star represents a period of renewal, the number's influence will help the individual obtain respite from their struggles.

The number 17 guides you with insight. 17 asks us to be responsible and have compassion for others. Seventeen can bring peace and love. After leaving Calypso, the nymph who held him captive, Odysseus floated on a raft for 17 days. A Japanese haiku poem has 17 syllables. You need to use 17 muscles to smile. March 17th is St. Patrick's Day, celebrated around the world.

The Star is aligned with the 28th path on the Tree of Life. Tzaddi or Ayin (Fishhook) is the 28th path within the Tree of Life and the 18th letter of the Hebrew Alphabet. This path connects Netzache (Victory) and Yesod (Foundation), relating to The Star card sense of calmness and renewal. You came through your struggles victorious and built strong foundations, which allows you to rest.

Tzaddi connects the spiritual realms to the material world. This path shows you how to serve others. It asks you to be your authentic self; give to others with an open and genuine heart. The 28th path brings new experiences. When you follow this path, you are creative and learn to move through the world without craving others' acceptance.

CHAKRA

The crown chakra (in Sanskrit called Sahasrara) is the seventh chakra, located at the top of your head. It is also called the thousand petal lotus chakra and considered a spiritual chakra. When your crown chakra is open and in balance, you feel alive and balanced. Life is full of pleasure and joy. The crown chakra is connected to the first chakra, as they are opposites in the chakra system.

The Crown Chakra is correlated with the bliss of pure consciousness. When you let go of your ego, you are accessing the Crown chakra.

The Sahasrara chakra is violet and shown as a lotus flower with a thousand petals. This chakra allows people to move beyond materialism to connect with the universe. Opening your crown chakra brings spiritual insight and self-confidence.

The crown chakra is the seventh chakra, and it is at the crown of your head connecting us with the universe and the Divine source of creation. You experience unity and the understanding that we are all connected; there is no separateness. This is where the mystical resides.

The crown chakra helps us transcendence our limitations and overcome our fears.

CORRESPONDENCES

- **Astrology:** Aquarius
- **Rune:** Laguz or Water: indicates the healing power of renewal
- **I Ching:** Hexagram 30 Clinging Fire: clarity Success comes from keeping your inner life strong and doing what is right. Be tender and flexible
- **Symbol:** Eight-pointed star
- **Animal:** Ibis
- **Element:** Air

~

READING CARD PLACEMENT

The Star card is about rest, hope, and guidance. You are being offered a period of calm and balance, a chance to rejuvenate. You may have experienced struggles, but now you can relax. You've hung in there and made it. Whatever issues have come to you in the past, The Star offers you hope. You can impact others as you feel peace and are able to be generous with your spirit.

Past

You had struggles and problems, but you were resilient. You gathered your strength and faced it all. You have learned and now you can relax and recover. It is time to refocus.

Present

A card of hope, the Star card is promising you a time out. You have a time of regeneration, and that will allow for positive outcomes. Stay resilient but allow yourself to relax and enjoy the peace. When you feel the moment is right to continue on, you will know it. Life is good and will continue to be good. Take the time to work on your spiritual self.

Future

You may be experiencing difficulties right now, but relief is coming. Keep up your strength, for all will work out. The Star card indicates that you will achieve your goal. When all is complete you will be able to rest and enjoy. The outcome is promising.

YES / NO KEY INTERPRETATION

The Star is a symbol of hope and renewal. The answer is yes.

KEYWORDS

Hope, faith, rejuvenating.

19

THE MOON

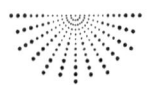

A full moon lights up The Moon card, a symbol of dreams and intuition. The moon's light is not as bright or warm as the sun, but it still guides us through the night so we can create our dreams in the daylight. The Moon card highlights our dreams and provides the energy to develop them into reality. It focuses on your creativity. The light it shines ensures that our work is not in vain but attainable and worthy. The Moon is there to guide you to the correct path.

On The Moon card, a path leads the walker into the mountains in the distance. At the side of the path are a wild wolf and a tame dog who bay at the moon. They illustrate the 2 sides of all humans; wild and tame, desirous and distant, rebellious and harmonious. To seek the light, you must walk between the 2 and allow them to guide you. Neither one is bad nor negative. It's the 2 sides blended together that you need to become whole as you continue your journey. The 2 together create strength.

A lobster is hanging out in the pond, looking like he is seeking land. The water is your emotion and unconscious and the lobster is your ego. Two grey towers on either side of the card, show you how all issues have 2 sides. When you consider decisions, be aware of both sides. You are walking one path, but you can always move to either side or find a new path to achieve your goals. Use the Moon's light to guide you as you make your quest in life. Each tower will lead you to a different place. As you travel, remember to consult both your conscious and unconscious minds.

The Moon is often considered feminine, as it controls female cycles, birth, and creativity. Through your dreams and imagination your creativity blossoms and you can create art, breathe life into your relationships, and be open to new experiences. Still, the Moon card will show you when you are following an unproductive path, be it a relationship, job or other projects. Your beliefs can be off kilter, built on sinking ground, not a solid foundation. Don't be afraid if this is what The Moon card is showing you for it is saving you from trouble down the road. It is telling you to be realistic. Use your intuition, let go of your thoughts, and dive deep into the water of your unconscious.

Other names for the Moon card are:

- Artemis
- Selena
- Hecate
- Crescent
- Luna

NUMBER 18 SYMBOLISM

The Moon is card 18 in the Major Arcana. The number 18 symbolizes inspiration and creativity. It also indicates new beginnings, progress and intuition. In China, 18 is considered a very auspicious number and considered good luck. The Hebrew word for life (chai) has the value of 18.

In the Christian tradition, the number eighteen is symbolic of bondage. The Israelites were held in slavery for 18 years by their enemies, the Philistines. The Moon card says that if you don't face your delusions and let the light shine on your goals and desires, then you will be in bondage.

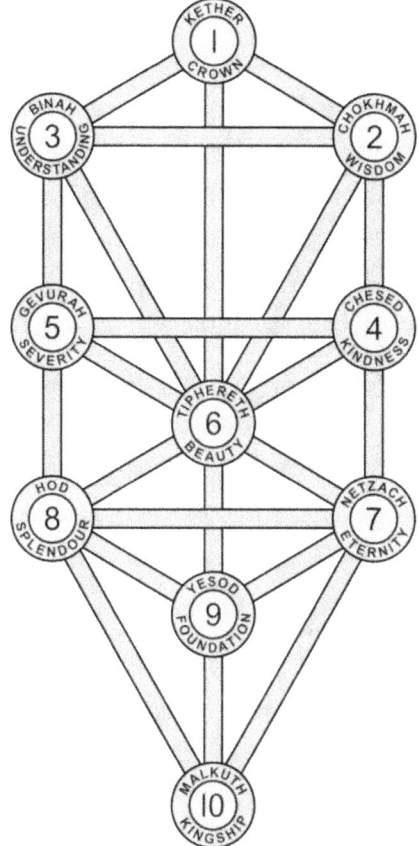

The Moon card walks the 29th Path, called Qoph (Back of Head). It runs from Netzach (Victory) to Malkuth (Kingdom) at the very bottom of the Tree and is considered the material world. It is also called Corporeal Intelligence. This path binds us to the earth. Qoph moves us from the spiritual to the earthly. It represents our unconscious and regulates our pleasure and fears.

As in The Moon Tarot card, the 29th path asks us to look at what we ignore and use the moon's light to show us our illusions. On this path intuition, and psychic abilities, seeds are planted. Path 29 is the path of healers and shamans.

CHAKRA

The Moon Tarot card is associated with the 6th Chakra, the Third Eye. The sixth chakra (Ajna in Sanskrit) uses intuition and the unconscious, instead of logic, to guide us, as does The Moon card. When using this Chakra, you gain knowledge of how you came to be where you currently are standing, your past and the impact of choices. Your intuition is developed, and you can see the world's true reality and people in it. Your blinders are taken off as you walk this path. The 6th Chakra is located between the eyebrows in the center of your forehead. It allows you to balance both inner and outer worlds.

The Ajna chakra brings you clear thinking, self-reflection, along with an understanding of where you want to be, who you want to be with, and want you want to do. It gives you spiritual depth. This spiritual grounding helps you move through the world with confidence. You have no illusions but feel sure your path is clear. Your faith in yourself grows and you can blend your intuition with your logical thoughts. Your third eye chakra observes the world from a distance, allowing your spirit and intuition to evaluate and add to the flow. Out of this comes wisdom and growth.

CORRESPONDENCES

- **Astrology:** Pisces. Jupiter is the ruling planet

- **Rune:** Algis or Elk indicates protection, a shield, defense, a shield. Wards off evil
- **I Ching:** Hexagram 60 Limitations: restrictions. Limitations and restrictions are not bad. They set the boundaries of your moral code. They allow you to function within reasonable constraints and not ruin yourself
- **Symbol:** The Moon
- **Animal:** Wolf or dog
- **Element:** Water

∽

READING CARD PLACEMENT

The Moon guides us to deal with our fears and to confront our delusions. Allow yourself to be open and be ready to change. This card strips away your illusions and shows you the truth of situations. Shining on reality, The Moon asks you to use your intuition and to trust your gut. Your fears may not be real, and your job is to balance your unconscious and conscious thoughts into what is real.

Past

In the near past you may have allowed your fears or other people's input to interfere in defining your path. The Moon shown light on that and showed what to let go of and now to move into the light.

Present

The Moon is shining its light on your dreams and goals. It could be that this goal or part of the goal is not realistic or has some obstacles attached to it that you weren't aware of. This can cause angst because your world is changing, and you have to do some deep thinking to realign your life. Use this time as an opportunity for self-reflection. Recreate yourself using your intuition and straighten the path ahead of you.

Future

You will be given the opportunity to bring one of your dreams into fruition. Take time now to evaluate these goals and ensure they are realistic. Let The Moon's light shone on the path ahead and allow it to help you adjust and make changes.

YES / NO KEY INTERPRETATION

The Moon is telling you to reflect and look carefully. The answer is not yes or no, either outcome is possible but make sure it is what you want.

KEYWORDS

Illusions, dreams, illumination, change, intuition.

20

THE SUN

The Sun card, number 19 in the major arcana, tells of success and achievement. Optimism abounds, and you can expect improvements and joy.

The sun is the source of life on earth. Without the sun's warmth, plants will not germinate, and the green lushness of our world would disappear. When the sun shines, humans feel happier and content. When it disappears behind the clouds, energy is reduced. Under the sun, everyone is rejuvenated.

A large, bright sun shines down on the earth, dominating the card. It has a human face as if to say it is one with us. The Sun gives energy and life. It is a card of fulfillment. It comes to you after the darkest of nights proclaiming, its strength and joy.

On the left-hand side of the card, sunflowers are growing tall. These four sunflowers represent the four suits of the Minor Arcana (Wands, Pentacles, Swords, and Cups) and the four elements (water, earth, air, and fire). A naked excited child sits on a white horse with a large red banner unfurled behind it. The child is delighted and demonstrates the joy of living life as your authentic self. The white horse on which the child sits is a sign of strength and pureness. The red flag represents passion and vitality.

With nothing to hide, the child shows you how maintaining balance with alignment to your values gives joy and energy. The Sun may be speaking of your life in general, your family, work, or other relationships. It is a powerful card and when it appears in a reading is always a positive omen.

The Sun card can indicate a positive outcome for a project or goal. It can also represent a marriage, a birth, or a promotion. Whatever you are dealing with at the moment, you will find it easier to handle. Your energy will attract others to you, and they may also help advance your goal. As you grow to trust this energy, your self-confidence will grow. The Sun is a card of good luck.

The Sun is a card of truth, balance, and harmony. The Sun comes to shine its light and reveal truth.

Other names for The Sun card are:

- Apollo; god of archery, truth, dance
- Helios, Titan god of the sun

NUMBER 19 SYMBOLISM

The Sun is number 19 in the Major Arcana and associated with success and honor. This number is filled with joy and happiness; thus, it is the perfect number for The Sun card.

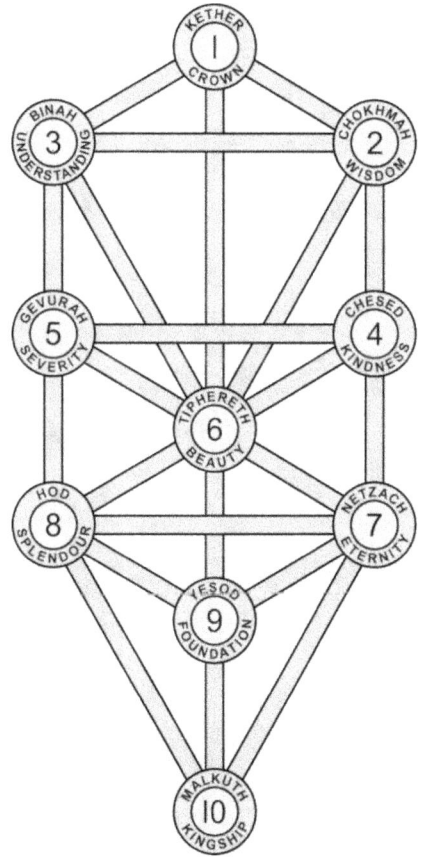

Number 19 is fascinating. It is known as a number of surrenders, as in surrendering to the universe. Nineteen represents completion; a project, a relationship, a job, or a pregnancy that will take you to a new beginning. A chapter from your life has ended or is nearing its end with new opportunities appearing that will take you to success. You are starting again, new projects are on the horizon, and the Sun gives you the energy to proceed forward and seize these opportunities.

The number 19 is a reminder to take care of yourself and proceed forward to grasp the advantages that are being presented. Having a positive attitude while you work will assist you and draw people to you. You can serve the people who are drawn to you, but they may also be beneficial to you. By helping others, you spread the joy of the Sun card.

The Sun is on the 19th pathway on the Tree of Life with the Hebrew name of Resh, meaning Head. The path connects Hod (concentrated mind) and Yesod (spirit). The path of Resh applies the powers of the Sun to your life and goals. This is the Path of science which shines a light to show us the truth. Resh moves your thoughts from the earthly plane to the spiritual zone and gives you unlimited potential.

CHAKRA

The Sun is associated with the third chakra, the Solar Plexus Chakra, Manipura, meaning shining gem. Located in the solar plexus area, near your diaphragm, it is the 3rd chakra from the bottom. It is illustrated by a golden yellow circle with 10 petals. In the middle is a triangle pointing down. This chakra deals with your willpower and having a sense of purpose in the world.

It also works with your ego. With this chakra, you can move into action and meet your challenges to move forward. And like The Sun, the chakra requires balance. Balance in using your power, balance in your emotions, and dealing with the people around you. Power doesn't mean power over others; it means your ability to control your thoughts and feelings and use them in positive life-enhancing ways.

Your solar plexus chakra is working whenever you exert self-control. When you have self-control, The Sun appears, using its light to guide you. Use this energy to gain the courage to move forward, know The Sun is predicting a positive outcome. When the sun shines, you hold your head high, shoulders back, and take deep breaths. This activates the solar plexus chakra, and it will assist you in your challenge.

The solar plexus chakra aids you in following your true path and remembering your values. It also helps you have an awareness of the world around you and guard against those things that can pull you away from your values and beliefs. Your ability to achieve your goals is held in the solar plexus chakra.

CORRESPONDENCES

- **Astrology:** Leo. Sun. Mars is the ruling planet
- **Rune:** Sowilo or Sun: indicates guidance, wholeness, success
- **I Ching:** Hexagram 30 Li: Flaming Beauty. clarity. Success comes from keeping your inner life strong and doing what is right. Be tender and flexible
- **Symbol:** The Sun
- **Animal:** Horse
- **Element:** Fire

～

READING CARD PLACEMENT

The Sun card represents success, abundance, and radiance. Like the sun itself, it gives strength and vitality to all those who feel its warmth. Joy and happiness are coming to you. You are currently able to aid others and be a role model. You are exuding positive, warm energy, and people feel your relaxed confidence. You are in a position to share your knowledge and gifts with others without expectations.

Past

Your past achievements have helped you get to where you are today and are the foundation for more positive outcomes. You can strengthen those outcomes by being true to yourself and carrying The Sun's energy with you into the future.

Present

When the Sun appears in your present placement, it's a positive sign. Your goals and desires will come true, providing you great benefit. The Sun will work with you as long as you put the energy in as well. If you are starting a new project, relationship, or adventure, the Sun is a positive influence.

Future

Soon you will be able to change your life and achieve your goals. Use your skills and to work towards your goals and prepare for this upcoming favorable period in your life. Put the hard work in now, for soon, you will be able to relax and enjoy your achievements.

YES / NO KEY INTERPRETATION

The answer is yes. The Sun is a card full of energy and positive outcomes.

KEYWORDS

Success, achievement, positive outcomes warmth, joy.

21
JUDGEMENT

The Judgement card shows the Archangel Gabriel, blowing a trumpet, calling people forward to be judged. The angel's large red wings rest on billowing gray clouds, contrasting with the blue sky. It's arms emerge to hold the trumpet. The trumpet has a square white flag with a red cross attached to it. The top half of the card is almost bright, with yellow hair, red winds, and gold trumpet, while the bottom half contrasts in shades of grey, black, and dull white.

At the sound of the trumpet, the graves of the dead open, and naked people, men, women, and children rise from their graves, arms spread, showing their compliance and willingness to be judged by the universe as they look up into the sky. They wish to find out if they will be raised up to heaven or not. A light will shine on all of their previous actions, and there will be where to hide.

The background is an extensive mountain range (some see it as a tidal wave), illustrating that you can't avoid Judgement. And this judgement is final for the Judgement card illustrates the last Judgement, the book of Revelation, and other mythologies. The people rising up will have their earthly actions weighed, to find out where they will spend the remainder of eternity: in heaven or in hell.

Judgement brings transition and change, but unlike Death or the Tower, it is not sudden change but change that springs from actions you have previously taken. Significant events are often about to take place when Judgement appears in a reading. Judgement can signal a major opportunity, one that will change your life, and you will need to act fast to take advantage of it, whatever it impacts your life. This is not to be taken lightly. What you choose to do at this fork in the road will affect the rest of your life. Don't waste too much time making the decision, or the opportunity will disappear. Use the knowledge you have accumulated over the years, check with your intuition, and trust your gut. Destiny is calling you, don't ignore its call.

Judgement appears when you are about to get an outcome in any situation, be it career, love, or relationships. Whether it is a positive or negative outcome depends on your actions to date, the values you have adhered to and the energy you have been putting into the world.

Judgement moves you from one situation to another such as the ending of a marriage or moving you from dating someone to marriage. It can mean a job promotion, a change in careers, or the end of job. Judgement shows you the results of the effort you have put in and whether is for better or worse.

The Judgement card is also called:

- The Aeon
- Prudence

NUMBER 20 SYMBOLISM

Judgement is card 20 in the Major Arcana, representing selflessness. When you are judged, part of your judgement will be based on your ability to put others in place of yourself and chose their needs over your own. Along with selflessness, 20 represents maturity and the ability to use that maturity for responsible actions.

The number 20 is also considered a number of communications, versatility and energy. On the tree of life, Judgement sits on Path 20 (Shin), between Hod and Malkuth. Shin is about changing, not only yourself, but everything around you. It represents Judgement, the day when all of us is exposed to the light. There is no more hiding. It is time to look at your past and clear it out.

JUDGEMENT | 179

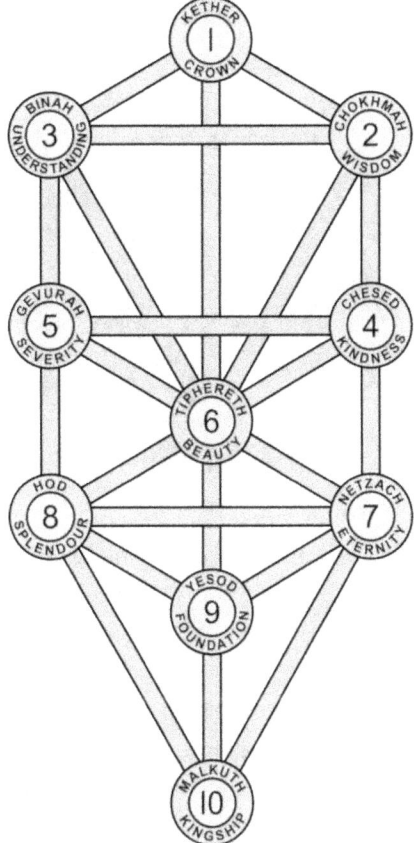

Heal any old wounds. It is not time to blame yourself or others, it is time evaluate so you can go forward with the knowledge gained from your mistakes.

Shin means tooth. Tooth speaks to our change process, where you break down, before building up again. Shin, in Hebrew, is shaped like 3 flames burning up. The flames purify and change your life. Others see the shape as columns and looking like a crown.

CHAKRA

The Crown chakra is the chakra of Divine Oneness and is called the 'thousand-petalled lotus.' It is pure consciousness and bliss. This energy center functions at its best we let go of our ego's need to be in charge.

Known as Sahasrara in Sanskrit, it is the seventh major chakra, located on the crown of the head and associated with spirituality. The Sahasrara chakra is violet and shown as a lotus flower with a thousand petals. This chakra moves people from their materialistic desires to connect with the universe and all in it. Opening the crown chakra brings spiritual insight, connection to your unconscious, and the ability to live with quiet self-confidence in all aspects of life.

The crown chakra is the seventh chakra and connects us with the universe and the source of creation. This chakra allows you to experience unity and understand that everything is connected at a fundamental level. The crown chakra is where mystical experiences emerge. You don't 'think' with the crown chakra or intellectualize your experiences. You just know. Serenity appears along with peace and joy. Your unconscious brings forth thoughts into your consciousness, and you know that life has depth and order.

CORRESPONDENCES

- **Astrology:** Scorpio. Pluto and Saturn are ruling planets
- **Rune:** Tiwaz: Tyr, the sky god
- **I Ching:** Hexagram 63 Chi Chi: After Completion
- **Symbol:** Trumpet
- **Animal:** Cat, sometimes Whale
- **Element:** Fire

READING CARD PLACEMENT

When the Judgement card arrives in your Tarot reading, it is time to take a stand and commit to your values. Your past actions are examined and if you need to change your path, you are given the opportunity. Clarify where you have been and where you want to go. Face your issues and responsibility.

Past

You experienced a time of reflection on your actions and values. You had a choice to make. You decided which path to follow and that decision will now follow you into the future.

Present

When Judgement appears in your present position, it asks you to reflect and evaluate yourself, past actions, and motives. It is time to face what you have done and to learn from your mistakes (if any). Take this opportunity to awaken yourself and grow. The Judgement card gives the chance to close doors on projects and lifestyles that no longer work for you. You can change your path in life. You may need to make small or large revisions to your life to facilitate these changes. Let go of the past and move towards the future.

Future

The time is coming when you will be asked to evaluate your actions. Start the process now to ensure that the Judgement will not be harsh. Make the changes you need. Be kinder, more flexible, and easier, on yourself and others. Make an accounting of your values. Do they still suit you and your goals? If not, don't wait for the future. Start the process now of identifying how you want to be in the world.

YES / NO KEY INTERPRETATION

The answer is yes, as long as you stick to your values and don't lie to yourself.

KEYWORDS

Reflection, change, awakening, newness, Judgement.

22

THE WORLD

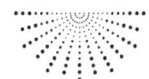

The World card depicts a naked woman wrapped in a long scarf, her hair is braided and full of jewels, dancing above the earth. She is inside a laurel wreath, a sign of triumph. On the 4 corners of the card are 3 animals, an eagle, lion, bull, and a man. These 4 represent the Zodiac signs: Leo, the lion, Taurus, the bull, Aquarius, the water bearer, and Scorpio, the eagle. They also symbolize the four elements, the four suits of the Tarot, four compass points, four seasons, and the four corners of the Universe.

The woman looks over her shoulder to her past, but her feet take her to the future. She carries two wands, symbolizing that the manifestation created with the Magician is now completed. As she dances, she illustrates balance, changing forces of life and the triumph of meeting your highest goals.

The circular wreath symbolizes the cycle of life; you complete a path and then begin a new one. Winter comes but then spring, and we begin anew. The laurel wreath is bound by a red infinity ribbon, reminding us of how life changes and shifts. You will continue to be rewarded and the cycle of life will continue to provide you with new projects and destinations. The spirit of this victory will follow you to your next dream.

Her legs are crossed in the same triangle pose as the Hanged Man but in this case, an upright triangle. While The Hanged Man speaks of waiting and suspension, The World's crossed legs are telling you to move forward. Take action and move to another project, follow your dreams.

When The World appears in your reading, it is an encouraging and life-enhancing message. You have grown, shown balance and understanding, and The World is rewarding you. Your unconscious and conscious mind are united, presenting you with joy and peace. Right now, you are allowing the situation you are in to flow and do what it must without any angst or lack of confidence. You know that whatever it brings, you will handle it with grace and balance. You have matured and feel secure in your knowledge. You are open to learning more and changing but have a deep internal sense that whatever comes your way, you can cope with it.

Other names The World card is known by are:

- Universe

NUMBER 21 SYMBOLISM

According to numerology, 21 is a creative spirit combined with pragmatism. Just as The World represents the combining of your unconscious thoughts and external desires. Twenty-one works through any conflicts with confidence and looks to compromise to maintain balance. The energy of 21 is positive and outgoing and tends to attract attention for the joy it exudes and the diplomacy it uses to come to decisions.

Because of its creative spirit 21 attracts artists and artistic endeavors of any type. It also contains the harmony of creation.

If you repeatedly see the number 21, you are experiencing the end of a cycle or project and are moving towards a new one. Twenty-one indicates that you have come to the end of a phase or project, and it is giving you energy for the new ones that will arrive. You are starting something new with all the knowledge, confidence, and power that you have accumulated. Pay attention when you see 21, what in your life is changing?

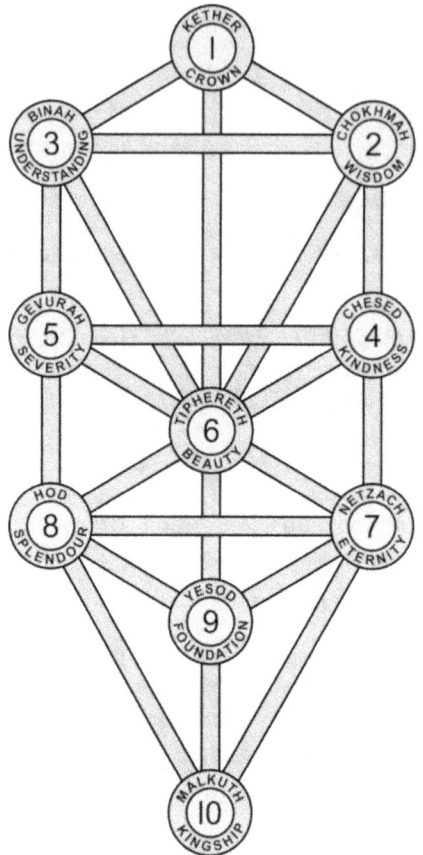

The World card is on the 22nd path on the Tree of Life, called Tav, meaning cross. Tav is the last letter of the Hebrew word emet, which means 'truth'. It is found between Yesod (Ethereal Realm) and Malkuth (Physical Realm). This path is symbolic of harmony and balance, bringing the spiritual to the physical and creating balance. Everything works on this path; there is agreement and unity. Tav also represents our destiny and completion.

CHAKRA

An earth element, the Root Chakra is the first chakra. The Sanskrit name for the root chakra is Muladhara, symbolized by a red lotus with four petals. The root chakra gives you the feeling of safety and a sense of being grounded. It's at the base of the spine and lays the foundation for expansion in your life. The first chakra is associated with security, your basic needs, and gives you the grounding for our life.

The Root Chakra, like The World, brings you stability. But it is also instinctual. You don't need to think; it is part of who you are as a human, primal in nature. The Root Chakra rules your physical needs such as food, water, and shelter. Think of Maslov's hierarchy of needs. One can't function well in life unless these basic needs are first met. It also warns us of danger, both physical and psychological. Red is a warning color, and The Root Chakra instinctively kicks in when it feels we are encountering difficulties.

The root chakra, when balanced, creates the foundation of security. It is the foundation on which we build our life and allows us to feel safe as we explore our universe. Like The World card, the root chakra gives us wisdom. It provides your ability to trust while you are out in the world.

This chakra oversees your sexuality and the urge to procreate. When the Root Chakra is balanced, the energy flows, and you feel secure and trusting. We can then use The Emperor's guidance and leadership to plan for our goals and dreams.

CORRESPONDENCES

- **Astrology:** Capricorn. Saturn
- **Rune:** Hagalaz: Hail or hailstone, when drawn indicates disruption, change, destruction and incredible power
- **I Ching:** Hexagram 64 Before Completion. Good fortune. Let your light shine
- **Symbol:** Globe or laurel wreath
- **Animal:** Lion
- **Element:** Earth

~

READING CARD PLACEMENT

The general meaning attached to the World card is fulfillment, achievement, and completion. It is a card of triumph and completion. The world is yours. Deep joy and happiness.

Past

Placed in the past, the World reminds you of all you have accomplished and encourages you to move forward. Change is constant, and you can build on previous successes. Set a new goal, don't rest on your laurels. Adapt and go with the flow. You have matured, and you can handle any obstacles that appear in the present. Your foundation is strong.

Present

A primary goal in your life is positively reaching completion. This may be a project, the birth of a child, marriage, retiring from a job, or any major goal in your life. With this completion comes change and movement to a new goal. You are approaching a new way of being in the world. Live your dreams and don't allow insecurity to stop you.

Future

Accomplishments are at hand if you stick to it and remember that change is constant. The world gives you the resilience to meet your goals despite any obstacles or challenges you may encounter on the path. Keep your dreams alive, you will succeed.

YES / NO KEY INTERPRETATION

The answer is yes but remember the world changes. The tide ebbs and flows and your dance with life should flow with it. You will have success and fulfillment.

KEYWORDS

Celebration, attainment, success, happiness, balance, fulfillment, achievement, self-awareness.

PART III
THE MINOR ARCANA

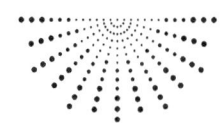

The Minor Arcana cards illustrate everyday events that have, are, or will take place in your life. The Minor Arcana consists of 56 cards in 4 suits: Wands, Cups, Swords, and Pentacles. Along with the 4 court cards: Page, Knight, Queen, and King, there are 10 numbered cards, Ace to 10. Some decks call the Page the Princess and the Knight the Prince. Their meanings remain the same.

The Minor Arcana suits correspond to the 4 elements:

- Wands: Fire
- Cups: Water
- Swords: Air
- Pentacles: Earth

The Minor Arcana follows a path from the Ace to the King. Generally, they speak of the journey from youth, or the beginning of a new direction, to the growth of a seasoned individual who understands the road they are on.

Minor Arcana cards can be shifted, moving from one position to another, or indeed, changing into another card based on your response to the situation or event. If the card you see in a reading is disturbing to you, then you can shift it by shifting your actions and attitudes.

Nothing is written in stone when it comes to the Minor Arcana.

1
WANDS

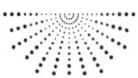

Wands are also known as Rods, Lances or Scepters, in some decks. Astrologically, Wands are associated with the fire signs of Aries, Leo, and Sagittarius.

Wands represent physical action connected to the element of Fire. Fire illustrates energy. Wands deal with creativity and the power required to achieve your dreams. They also deal with your career – not the financial aspect but the actual work that you choose to do. A Wand card, depending on placement, can indicate travel and forward movement. Traditionally, Wands are considered masculine, but this is an older sexist representation when the view of women was of passive and non-athletic beings. When you see a male on a tarot card, it is easy to shift the image to a female or non-binary person.

Wands are powerful but they require your hard work to earn rewards. According to Crowley, the Wand suit, Aces to Pages, represent the continent of Asia.[1] Wands drive your goals and projects and require you to take action, to do something.

Ace of Wands

This card is telling you to become active. You will learn your answers through movement, doing almost anything. Use your energy to spark a new endeavor or solution. You are receiving gifts from the universe. Opportunities are presenting to you. This card bodes well for any start you are making. Take risks and begin new projects.

Two of Wands

The individual on the card is gazing out to sea, looking for his ships to come in. You have great expectations of your life or current project. Keep focused, enthusiastic, and use your strength to move forward. Feed the flames of your fire. If you haven't already, formulate your goals and visualize success. The Two of Wands is a favorable card to receive when you are working on your visions. You sent the ships out, and in time, you will reap the rewards.

Three of Wands

Your ship is nearing. Put in additional effort, and you will gain what you seek. Be clear of your goals, so you don't waste time. Collaborate with others on your journey; it is not the time to go it alone. Your productivity and efforts have created gains, so continue on the path. Don't stop now when you are close to achieving your goal. Remember that your character is your brand in life, don't deviate from your values. When your goals are so close keep your faith and belief in the positive realm. Avoid all negativity and encourage not only yourself but others.

Four of Wands

Small victories are appearing. The 4 of Wands is a positive card, showing that you are creating the right foundations for success. Be authentic, and more will come to you. Celebrate what you have already achieved, even if it's small steps. There will be continued successes, but joy in the present gives gratitude. And gratitude brings forth more success. The 4 of Wands card can indicate family happiness as well as prosperity in your career. Don't let doubt shadow your continuing efforts for you are being blessed and loved. Encourage yourself and others to proceed as planned.

Five of Wands

You are in conflict. It may be time to take some time for yourself. You can't help others when your soul is drained of energy. Consider where you'd like to go next and what changes need to happen in your life.

When confronted with obstacles and competition, it is time to refocus your path. You are fighting hard but perhaps not in the right areas. Regrouping will help you gain the knowledge and insight you need right now.

Six of Wands

Victory and success come to you through hard work. You are developing leadership skills and understand that acknowledging your weaknesses makes you stronger. Go after your goals.

The six of wands is riding triumphantly home, having conquered and succeeded. You are moving to success and to finding solutions to any issues you encounter. This is a glorious time, enjoy it and continue to grow. However, don't rest on your laurels. Be a leader with empathy and compassion to ensure you continue to be blessed with success.

A project you are working on is coming to success.

Seven of Wands

Obstacles have appeared, and you may be struggling to deal with confrontation. This card deals with your actions, and the more open you are with others, the better it will be.

Still, protect yourself and use your knowledge wisely. You are on the right path, stand your guard and defend what is right. Hold firm and believe in yourself. Consult with others.

Eight of Wands

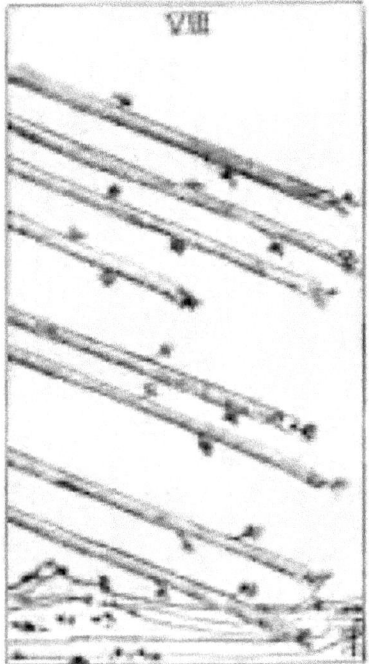

Number 8 is a lucky number. Take action. Achievement is in sight, or perhaps you already have it in hand. There could be good news. You may be clearing out the clutter of your life. Listen to others and work to understand their needs. Doing this will aid you in gaining your goal, for as you connect with them, the energy flows back to you. Good luck is coming your way, and things are moving fast. It is time to grab life and engage energetically.

Nine of Wands

You have gone through a struggle but can't quite believe it is over. So, you stand on guard, waiting, using your intuition to anticipate what may be on the horizon. Learn to accept yourself and your accomplishments. The 9 of Wands gives a final burst of energy to see you over the line. Look within to find your courage and the ability to finish the race. You'll get there. Protect yourself but be assured that the universe is watching out for you.

Ten of Wands

You feel burdened with much responsibility. You may be close to burnout and feel oppressed. The card indicates it is time to refresh yourself. Talk to others, share your concerns. Look for ways to make it easier on yourself. Put something aside while you work on one goal.- Take a look at what lies in front of you and prioritize your work. Learn to take breaks. If you are exhausted, you can't to work or help others.

Page of Wands

A quick thinker, the Page of Wands is telling you to be open-minded. Don't close your mind to new ideas. News is coming your way, which at first may seem off-putting. But sit with the information. Often what we first think is unfortunate turns into good. Maintain your motivation and continue your work, keeping in mind that good news is coming.

Use your intuition and your mind to consider all aspects of your situation.

Knight of Wands

You are thinking about your career or using your creativity. Use this energy to help others. The power of the Knight of Wands will aid. Find projects that speak to you and propel you into a mission that aids many. When you use the energy of the Knight of Wands, you gain momentum and force. Charge forward. Don't be reckless, as that can lead to issues later on. Hold yourself back from immediately reacting to others or situations.

Queen of Wands

The Queen provides insight and is the ultimate in self-confidence. Take control of your life and believe in yourself but consider the other person's side. Create new goals by thinking differently. You have the energy and strength to create what you need. The Queen of Wands tells you to not have an out, a back-up plan, but rather move forward with the full confidence that you are going to succeed.

King of Wands

You are receiving opportunities. Don't let them slip away. Be tenacious and ready to fight for your beliefs. You are in charge. Channel your King of Wands. You need his grounded authority and skills right now. There may be a person around you, a mentor or a guide, who reflects the qualities of the King of Wands. Take command. Look for new ideas to incorporate into your goals. Let the King of Wands make things happen for you.

2
CUPS

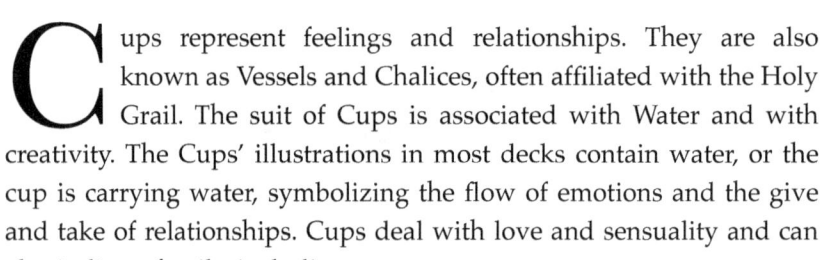

Cups represent feelings and relationships. They are also known as Vessels and Chalices, often affiliated with the Holy Grail. The suit of Cups is associated with Water and with creativity. The Cups' illustrations in most decks contain water, or the cup is carrying water, symbolizing the flow of emotions and the give and take of relationships. Cups deal with love and sensuality and can also indicate family, including pregnancy.

Intuition is also connected with the Cups, allowing the expression of your unconscious. Listen to your gut as the Cups guide you in your creativity and defining your talent. Additionally, Cups deal with healing, both emotionally and physically. If you are cleansing, let the Cups work with you.

This suit of cards speaks of various transformations that take place in your life. According to Crowley, Cups, Aces to Pages indicate the Pacific Ocean.[1] Cup cards oversee your heart.

Ace of Cups

The Ace of Cups signifies coming abundance. It could be the beginning of a new relationship. A possible love affair or a renewal of your existing relationship. This love is balanced. Open up and allow it in. Your wisdom will guide you. If this card appears at the beginning of a new relationship, it bodes well for you and your partner. The Ace of Cups represents the seeding of love.

Two of Cups

Friendship or falling in love. Creative blessings. The Two of Cups brings love and the healing power of love. You may have found someone to be a partner in a business, romantic, or other relationship, with each of you providing different strengths. The Two of Cups tells you the relationship will be equal, a true partnership, full of cooperation.

Three of Cups

A joyous celebration. Friendship and pleasure. Enjoy the love that surrounds you – friendships, lovers, children, and family. You have goodness in your life; express gratitude that you are blessed in this way. Call someone, have a party, treat a work colleague to a coffee. Share your blessings. Abundance flourishes and grows when it is shared.

Four of Cups

A feeling of being stuck. You may need to withdraw to regain energy. Take a spiritual retreat. Nurture yourself and all that you value about yourself. Go inward, become introspective and consider who you are. Make a list of your values, your attributes, and what you value about yourself. If something needs to change, make the change, and move forward. Don't beat yourself up over it. Move to the positive and commit to the change.

Five of Cups

Grief appears with a feeling of loss. You may have been betrayed or disappointed in a relationship. To overcome this, look beyond to where you can let go of your hurt and open your heart. Change in life is an ongoing experience and newness will enter. You fill find new love, more friends, or an outstanding job opportunity. Grieve but don't remain stuck.

Six of Cups

Fond memories that provide pleasure. You may be remembering your childhood or other earlier days. Someone may return to you that you haven't seen for a while. You are integrating your past mistakes and successes. You carry with you all the joy and delight of the past. This card is a very fertile card and one of the best cards to receive in a Tarot reading.

Seven of Cups

You risk being taken in by an illusion. Several possibilities are before you, some seductive and too good to be true. The opportunities are both tempting and confusing. It is best to retreat and wait to see which of them plays out. Are you happy or are you missing something? Reach out for those things that matter and fill your soul.

Eight of Cups

Something in your life has come to completion – a relationship, a job, or a way of being. Don't look for blame as this is a normal life change. You have a new path to travel as you follow your heart. Consider the spiritual aspects of your situation. Go forward, knowing this is right. Your intuition is telling you whether to go left, right, or straight ahead. Trust yourself.

Nine of Cups

Success! A goal is achieved, or a long-term desire or wish has come to fruition. Happiness surrounds you, and you are content. Celebrate your gain and appreciate all the work and effort you put into achieving it. The Nine of Cups is another great card to receive in a reading. Happiness is of your own making. You can be happy in the smallest of places.

Ten of Cups

The ten of cups brings fulfillment. A happy family, a loving relationship, friends, and all the goodness of life are with you. Receiving this card in a reading brings blessings. Life is full of joy and magic. While you enjoy this love, along with the relationships it brings, remember to express gratitude and not take people for granted. All of this may not last, so feel blessed.

Page of Cups

Also known as the Princess. You may be at the beginning of a new project or relationship. You have dreams that you wish to fulfill. A baby may be on the way. The Page of Cups is a sweet person, full of fun and light-heartedness. Trust your heart as you are on the right path. Don't let day to day stresses cloud your vision as you go on your journey.

Knight of Cups

Also known as the Prince. Follow your dreams but be aware of reality. There may be obstacles. You can overcome, but only if you ground your solutions. The Knight of Cups can also represent love and a new relationship. Follow your heart, regardless of which area – creativity, romance. The Knight brings you the message that now is the time to open up to life.

Queen of Cups

The Queen of Cups represents a strong woman, either yourself or a woman in your life. She can inspire you. The card indicates bringing your dreams into reality. The Queen of Cups is nurturing and warm. Use her qualities to grow your dreams. Sit quietly, listening to your inner voice with faith. Be empathetic to others. Open your heart and take a risk.

King of Cups

The King of Cups indicates a spiritual path. A measured man, the King considers all obstacles to his goals and masters them. He is associated with the arts and culture and radiates love. Look for a person in your life who can provide this kind of support and at the same time, look within yourself for compassion. Attempt any task with a positive attitude.

3
SWORDS

An air element, the Swords suit cards deal with your mind. Swords govern intelligence and communication. They can indicate your level of stress and mental acuity. Swords are double-edged, meaning they are used for both good and harm. Whoever holds the sword can swing it either way.

Swords can also illustrate various authority figures in your life. These authority figures could be employers, government, judges, teachers, and others who influence you or aspects of your life. They may show conflict and ambition in your life.

Swords cut through illusions, displaying the truth. Through this truth, Swords bring light to your situations. Swords are sensitive to your path and your emotions. According to Crowley, the suit of Swords covers the Americas.[1] Swords assist in making decisions and help you to overcome obstacles. It is time to make plans.

Ace of Swords

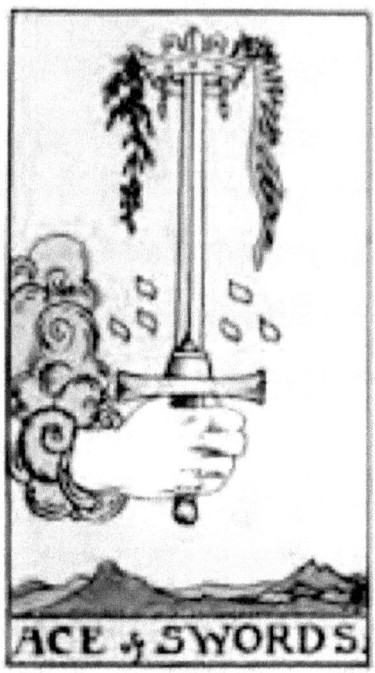

The Ace of Swords cuts both ways and helps you see through the fog, bringing clarity. You can now remove yourself from situations and people who no longer serve you, your values, and your goals. When the Ace of Swords appears, it may bring a current position to a head, forcing you to react and make a conquest. Think differently to see if you can change the outcome. Be valiant in your efforts.

Two of Swords

The Two Swords suggests that you are caught between two - two people, two views, or a split feeling. You need to resolve the issue peacefully. Don't procrastinate; instead, act with integrity and knowledge. Consider all possible compromises. Use your intuition, and you can resolve the issue in a fair way that pleases all involved. Find a peaceful solution that benefits all.

Three of Swords

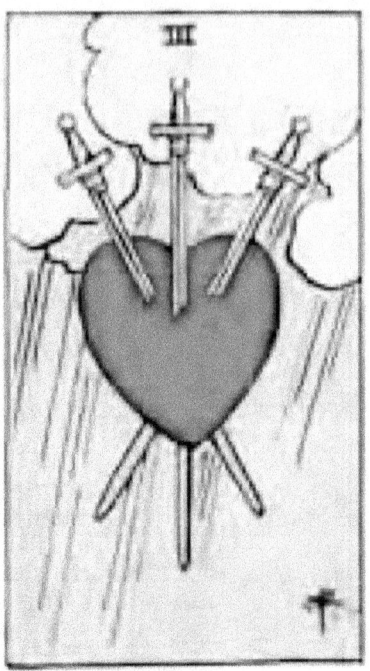

The Three of Swords is a heartache card. The pain is deep but work your way through it. It can take time but remember it will end. This kind of pain is often necessary to clear out your mind, leaving you aware of new ideas and ways in the world. You are losing something important and may feel down. It could be a lover, a marriage, your child leaving home, a job you love, or a friendship. Be kind to yourself. All grief heals in time.

Four of Swords

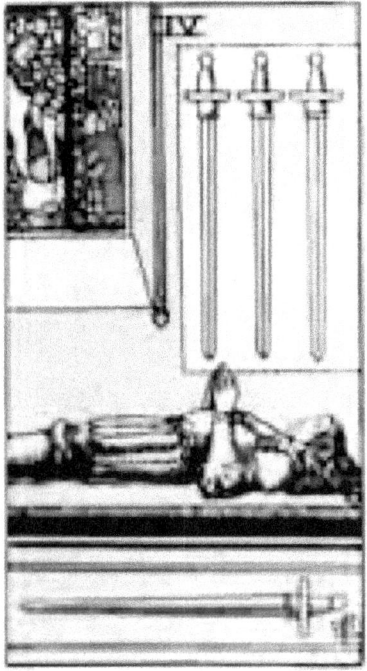

It is time to withdraw and seek solitude. Meditate, use your spiritual values to guide you. Rest and recover. Reflect on the past. Do what it takes to rejuvenate yourself: escape your current environment, pamper yourself, or just sit still, listening to your inner thoughts. Go within. Mentally, you are not at your best, take advantage of this time to heal yourself.

Five of Swords

Defeat. Communication between you and someone in your life has disintegrated into humiliation and loss. Check your actions and your words to make sure you aren't coming across as aggressive or angry. If you change your actions you may change the outcome. Step back and take a look at yourself. Corruption, on any level, only leads to further deterioration. Check your course and readjust your compass to ensure you are in line with your values.

Six of Swords

Take time to renew. Consider a holiday somewhere peaceful and calming. A new environment will give you a new perspective. The feeling in the Six of Swords is one of escape, leaving a struggle behind. When you choose to find a way to renew, it is best to leave all behind. Use intelligence, logic, and science to find your way. You may be making a pilgrimage.

Seven of Swords

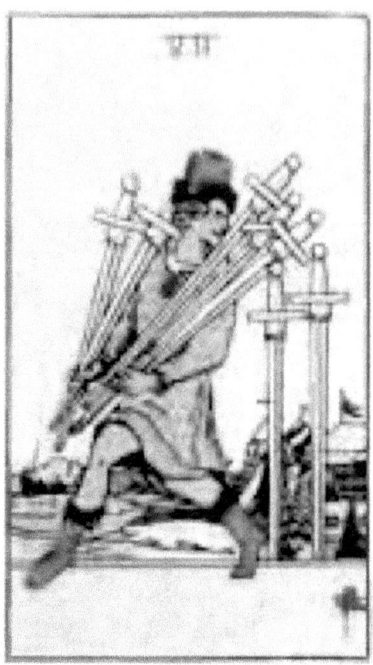

Use your intellect as you develop new ideas and face challenges. Change is normal and often leads to an amazing experience if you let it. There is deception around you, a sense of futility. Either you are trying to 'steal' something that doesn't belong to you, or someone is trying to take something of yours. Be careful and watch. Avoid deception.

Eight of Swords

You may experience the sensation of being trapped or a victim. Loneliness or anxiety invades your soul. Still, 8 signifies completion and the start of new things. Look around you and see that the swords which surround you may be of your own making. Grab fresh starts and new ideas; don't fear as some may be worth embracing. One of them may fit your life.

Nine of Swords

Suffering. A time of mental darkness, possible depression. You feel lost. You have the power to wake from this bad dream. A sense of cruelty hangs over the situation. There is a temptation to feel self-pity. Don't succumb. Sometimes things occur because the universe has an unseen goal. The swords on the card do not bind the woman. Take a look and see she is sitting there of her own accord. Use your intuition to calm yourself, then move forward.

Ten of Swords

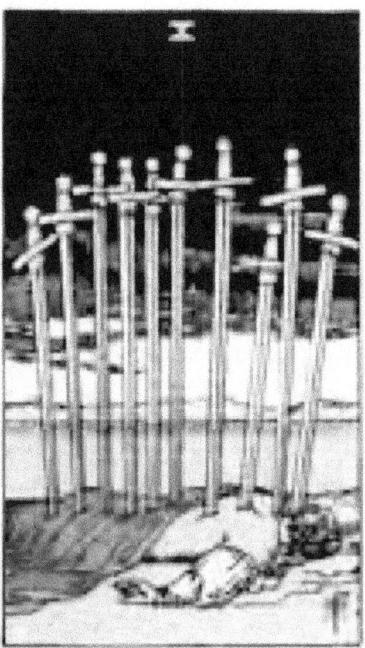

When this card appears in a reading, you may have been betrayed and want to seek revenge. You may have lost love or a job. Your career may be fading away. Whatever it is, it is ending. Sometimes called the true death card because it represents the death of something in your life. But death always brings life again. Snow covers the earth, plants die off but soon, the sun warms the ground, the snow melts, and new buds appear. All will resolve itself.

Page of Swords

Be objective, but curious. Be vigilant and stay aware of any challenge to your values. Someone may be hiding information from you, information that is vital to your plans. Be ready to act when the light is shines and understand how this information impacts you. Maintain your ambitions but keep your eyes open.

Knight of Swords

A change may be coming, opening up a new life for you. Can indicate a journey. Be aware of your surroundings and what is happening. Take the most direct path to your goals, and don't waste time or energy on other items. If you want to achieve something, you need to act. Life may present you with an opportunity, and if you waste time making a decision, it could be lost. Do your research quickly and charge forward.

Queen of Swords

The Queen of Swords is a strong independent woman who uses her charm to make her way. Very professional, executive type. Be objective to be successful. Receiving this card in a reading indicates good luck in any venture that involves communication. The Queen of Swords is an action woman. She researched and now wants to create movement. With her sword, she cuts through all the fog, creating a clear and concise path for you. The time is now.

King of Swords

A man of action, the King of Swords, is intelligent and makes sound judgements and decisions. He gives good advice. If you need to make a decision, turn to your inner King of Swords. He can debate with the best of them. You don't need to rush as The King encourages you to explore the possible outcomes of your decisions. Use your analytical skills.

4
PENTACLES

P entacles are associated with the material aspects of life and the earth element. Pentacles are also known as coins and disks. They generally show you information regarding your finances, economics, talent, and general wealth. They also may illustrate the security and stability level in your life and the foundation you have built to date. Pentacles can also deal with your health and body issues.

Pentacles are showing things that are long term. Where Cups tend to the unconscious aspect of life, Pentacles often denote the external pieces of life. These cards ask you to ground yourself, use your common sense, and not go off on fantasy or daydreams.

Pentacles, according to Crowley, cover the geography of Europe and Africa.[1]

Ace of Pentacles

A card of financial luck and success. Material benefits. A new contract or job offer. If you have been pondering an idea for a business or creative project, now is the time to launch. Make yourself open and available for the universe to bless you. An investment you've made could produce a small reward.

Two of Pentacles

Your wealth is growing – that could be money, material possessions, skills, or talents. You are juggling items or concerns in your life. Find a way to achieve balance. Notice how the juggler on the card controls the coins. They are not loose and running free but are banded in an infinite loop. The 2 of Pentacles can also indicate that you need to choose between 2 viable options. Change is on the horizon, and you can't avoid it.

Three of Pentacles

Building on your foundations. You are developing skills and are no longer a 'newbie.' You are moving upwards in your career or creative endeavors. People are beginning to notice you and ask for your particular skills. Your reputation is solid. Join a business association or other group that can help you build your project. Mingle and network to achieve the best results. Work is required, but you are capable of putting in the time and needed energy.

Four of Pentacles

Work on building your wealth or a business. You have the power to do so. Keep your foundation strong. Your skills are in demand. You are ready to reach tall and continue your gains. You are practicing being frugal, which can be a good thing. But ensure you aren't too cheap or miserly. Sometimes quality requires spending: money, time or energy. Don't withhold time spent with people to the point of injuring your relationships.

Five of Pentacles

Change is coming, and may indicate a loss. You may have become too independent and now need to reach out to others. None of us have achieved in isolation; we all have input from others. You need to seek out others for their assistance. Behind the desolate figures on the card is a church, and churches doors are always open. You are worrying, but an old saying is 'worrying is like a rocking horse, you can rock all day and never go anywhere.'

Six of Pentacles

The Six of Pentacles indicates you will give and receive benefits. You may be gaining profits or gifts. People are generous with you. And it may be time for you to be generous with others. Gratitude brings grace. Give and receive with your heart. If you are genuine, you will receive far more than give you away. Benevolent and anonymous charity brings its rewards, cheering your heart and soul. You may experience kindness from others.

Seven of Pentacles

Be patient and let things grow. Follow the harvest cycle. You first seed, then water and watch the growth. At the appropriate time, you harvest, prune, and get ready for the winter. And then it starts again. Be aware of where you are in the cycle. Don't try to harvest too soon, when you still need to be working, hoeing out the weeds. But also, don't let the harvest rot on the vine. It is time to promote yourself, so when the harvest is ready, others are aware.

Eight of Pentacles

Ongoing progress. Don't be overwhelmed by your whole goal. Instead, break it into smaller pieces so you can look at what you have achieved along the way. The 8 of Pentacles tells you to be proud of what you've achieved. There is always more to learn, so keep doing your best and not resting on your laurels. You have talent and are learning how to use it to your best ability. Look into apprenticing with someone more skilled than you.

Nine of Pentacles

Success and enjoyment of life. Good things come your way. You are enjoying material wealth but also good relationships. The woman illustrated on the card is happy in her garden. She has reached a state of contentment after hard work. Enjoy yourself. You have worked hard and earned it. All of these benefits are coming to you through your efforts. Share the prosperity acquired at this time, and your relationships will improve.

Ten of Pentacles

The Ten of Pentacles is a happy card. Blessings abound in your home and family life. Open yourself to these blessings and well-earned wealth. There is enough not only for yourself but for those around you. This strong foundation will carry you forward and will last. The Ten of Pentacles provides stability in life. When you have a strong foundation, you can sit quietly enjoying it, or you can work through your next moves to further improvements.

Page of Pentacles

Creativity. Happy news. News that can lead to new opportunities will appear to you. Take your vision and expand on it. Consider how you can turn a goal into reality. Think carefully. Be thoughtful. Don't rush ahead and waste your time on something that could turn out to be a dead end. Ensure that you investigate before proceeding. You may hear good news about an investment. Be practical.

Knight of Pentacles

    Nurture your practical qualities. Seek security. Be dependable. Develop new opportunities through hard work and focus. Be determined to succeed. Channel the qualities of the knight to see you through as you persevere to your goal. Now is the time to develop good habits that will see you through any difficult times. Practices like punctuality, being practical, kindness to others, and gratitude will aid you in future endeavors.

Queen of Pentacles

The Queen of Pentacles is a financially independent and well-organized woman. Take care of your possessions and your money. The Queen brings beauty and prosperity into your life. She is encouraging you and supporting you as you build your life. Not just in finances but in other areas as well – love, creativity, and career. The Queen of Pentacles is a charitable woman; learn from her.

King of Pentacles

The King of Pentacles is intertwined with nature. He is successful and wealthy. With this card in a reading, The King grants you a positive experience, blessing, and possibly wealth. He is a great resource, full of power. The King of Pentacles works hard for his success. He is on top of all his investments and enterprises. He understands the power of a single dollar and the responsibility of enormous wealth. Use him wisely.

PART IV
MULTIPLE CARDS

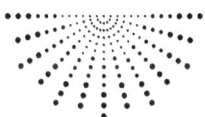

In a reading if several cards of a certain suit are laid out, it signifies:

- Wands: Change
- Cups: Love
- Swords: Mental Anxiety
- Pentacles: Intrigue or Financial Issues

There are times when multiple suits of the same numbered Minor Arcana cards appear in a reading. Depending on the number of multiples, where they land in the reading and the question asked, multiples can have different impacts.

1
ACES

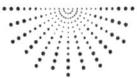

The Meaning of Multiple Aces

The word 'Ace' is from Middle English and Old French. In the Tarot, aces are typically low, and tens high. Aces are zero and ones, and yet incredibly valuable. Ace's carry potential and because of that, power in a reading. Whenever you see an Ace in a layout, be pleased.

Aces are situated at the beginning of each suit, introducing the suit, and giving an indication of the inherent meaning and energy of the suit. The Aces start your journey through their suit. Regardless of the suit, they represent focus and energy, along with new beginnings and opportunities. They set the tone of suit and can cover physical, emotional and mental activities in a reading.

Look at Aces as symbols of the Tarot energy represented by The Fool. They are number 0 and 1, the start of everything. The seeker fills the void of 0 by beginning the journey towards their future. Each suit is represented by their Ace and that suit indicates where you need to begin and where you may need to work to fill in the missing pieces. Because they are 0 or 1, there are boundless possibilities waiting for you to realize them.

Aces reside in Kether on the Tree of Life. Kether is the highest and purest of all the sefirot or emanations on the tree of life. Kether is closest to God and the source of all creation. When you look at the four Aces, you will see that each has a hand extending from a cloud, indicating spirit. Each hand gives a different offering, based on its suit. The gift offered is divine, from spirit and given to the seeker's life if they choose to accept it.

When an Ace appears in a reading, it signifies the beginning of something new. In single card draw or a three card reading, an Ace signals 'yes'.

- **Four Aces** are good luck bringing with them abundance and a good life. Four Aces in a reading means that the seeker will have many opportunities. Or possibly, a new environment is presenting itself. This can be overwhelming, but it will lead to growth and fulfillment. View many Aces as a positive portent in the seeker's life.
- **Three Aces**, mean that effort is required to bring it to the level of four Aces. You can achieve goals but it will require work.
- **Two Aces** in a reading may show a strong relationship with the potential of significant growth, possibly in more than one area of your life. Two Aces indicates more than one – more money, more love, more opportunities and growth.

All of the Tarot's energy can be accessed through the Aces. With four Aces you can achieve anything. Remember the elements associated with each suit – *Fire for Wands, Water for Cups, Air for Swords, Earth for Pentacles*. The Aces ignite these elements, creating the energy that begins the journey. The Aces give hope of new beginnings and fresh starts.

∼

2
TWOS

The Meaning of Multiple Twos

Twos are an illustration of combined forces in each Tarot suit. The reader must consider what occurs when two separate entities come together. Depending on the suits, the other cards in the layout, there are many answers to this question. Twos can be harmonious or cause disruption and a choice between separate parts. This separation can happen between 2 individuals, 2 businesses or within the individual seeker in their ideas or thoughts. Sometimes the separation is between 2 values and you need values clarification as to which value is the higher one, or how to merge the values and meet both goals.

When you identify conflict based on 2, don't assume this is a negative. Clarification can result in a positive outcome. It can clear out confusion for you, leading to a deeper development and growth.

Twos in the Tarot usually refer to decisions. A decision needs to be made or you have already made a decision which is now impacting your life. Occasionally, it can refer to a decision that two people are making together – for example a couple buying a house. But most often, it refers to the seeker and the question they are asking for the reading.

Making a decision can involve resolving the conflict between the heart and the head. It can also be about what is right versus what is wrong. Or perhaps it is about staying versus leaving (relationship, job, career, house).

Two is about balance and juggling between 2 opposites, like yin and yang, feminine and masculine, cold and heat. In fact, anything where there is an opposite. Two is also about partnership and thinking about the other. Two tests your ability to see the other person's point of view and stand in their shoes. Two is about give and take, learning to consider others and put them above your own desires on occasion.

Two is about learning that what you believe and value may not be the same as what others believe and value. You learn, through 2, that neither side is wrong and neither is right. It always depends on the situation and where the universe has put you at the moment in time. And, that different point of view can enhance your life, filling in missing pieces that give you additional guidance and paths to follow.

Two asks you to be diplomatic. To think about others and be flexible. That can also mean being diplomatic with yourself, for sometimes the conflict is internal and we must negotiate with ourselves to find inner peace.

Twos are in Chokmah on the Tree of Life. Chokmah means wisdom and is the second of the ten sefirot. It holds creation power and the ability to change your lives. This is energy in its pure form, a joining of two opposites.

Chokmah gives you insight, like flashes of light that come into your mind.

- **Four 2s** in a reading often mean there is conflict around you. Think of 'too many cooks spoil the broth'. You may be working with too many people on a project and need to pare it down. Or perhaps you are seeing too many people in a romantic sense, unwilling to commit to 1.
- **When three 2s** appear it can be the same confusion as four 2s, just a little bit calmer with fewer difficulties. There may

be a need to make a choice and this choice will come easier to you than with four 2s.
- **Two 2s** are about partnerships. This can be a business or romantic partnership. Or a joining of like minds to take on complete a project. Generally, these are good partnerships but still be mindful of balance. Twos require balance to ensure growth and happiness.

3
THREES

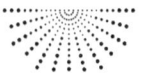

The Meaning of Multiple Threes

In the Tarot, 3s signify a unifying force. The number 3 is the natural outcome of the joining of two.

Three cards of all the suits reinforce the concepts of loyalty and moving to the point of no return. Threes tell the seeker to move on, let go of the past. The 3 cards are about setting boundaries and sticking to those boundaries. This may mean a total change – in lifestyle, in love, friends and other relationships.

Threes start the process of change. They don't finish it, but they take the outcome of 2s and make things happen. There is work to be done, actions to be taken and seeds to be sown.

The number 3 expresses the creative power of the universe. It is the combination of 1 and 2, and out of those joining forces comes the seekers next reality.

Threes are on the path between Binah (understanding) and Dalet (door). This path brings together wisdom and understanding to open the door to new realities. The path presents you with creative fertility. It is the gate to a new life, one that uses intuition and combines the aspects of two and one. This is a path for artists, for people to use their imagination but combine it with logic for balance.

Binah is feminine energy, the mother who receives the energy of Chokhmah, moving the creative actions to the open door of Dalet.

The first 3 paths on the Tree of Life are considered the foundational energies of the universe. Binah gives understanding. It takes the idea generated by 2 and gives it structure from 3.

Three is revered by many religions and cultures. It is considered a creative power. There is the Christian belief in the Father, Son and Holy Ghost. Hinduism has Brahma, Vishnu and Shiva. Time is represented as past, present and future. We are born, live a life and then die. All 3s.

The number 3 represents your manifestation of goals and the development of creative energy. It is dynamic and full of life. In the Minor Arcana, the 3s of all suits refer to creativity, growth and development. Threes create the momentum to move toward your goal. Your purpose has been defined; it is time to take action.

Threes also tell you that you are not alone. You bring with you the partnership of two, generating a team. Threes can mean childbirth and fertility, both physical and mental.

When you are on the path of 3, you may find yourself being distracted. If so, you will lose the energy through lack of focus. Stick to your goal, don't allow your energy to be dissipated through flitting off to other sparkly things.

- **Four 3s** in a Tarot card reading gives luck. Great things will happen if you work with others. Life at this point in time will go well.
- **Three 3s** in a Tarot card reading is also lucky. Keep yourself focused on your intent. Success will come at a slower pace than if you received 4 threes. Accept any offer of support.
- **Two 3s** give an energy burst but one that relies on you working strongly with others.

If you find yourself off course, go back to the foundations of the 2 and 1 to remind yourself of your original goals.

4
FOURS

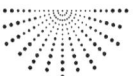

The Meaning of Multiple Fours

Four is a number of stability, practicality, and consolidation. Four has its own power. It is peaceful but also can indicate avoidance, especially where you are avoiding the inevitable. Fours speak to holding firm to your path. Keep yourself grounded.

Fours are everywhere:

- 4 suits in the Tarot deck
- 4 seasons on earth
- 4 Elements: Water, Earth, Fire, Air
- 4 Seasons: Winter, Spring, Summer, Fall
- 4 Directions: North, South, East, West

Four is solid keep you grounded to the earth while supplying confidence. Without 4, it is easy to get lost or distracted from your goal. Four gives structure.

The 4th sephiroth is *Chesed* or kindness. This kindness is one of grace, allowing you to create a vision of how your life will move forward. As with 4s, it requires balance and looking inward to ensure you understand where you are and where you'd like to be.

Four is a balancing number. When you are out of sync, 4s bring you back to the ground, balancing your energy. Fours allow you to see that you have what it takes to obtain your goal, as long as you put in the work and the right energy. Four brings calmness along with a sense of direction.

- **4 fours** received in a tarot reading indicate life is full of contentment. Your life will be stable and flow easily for the next while as shown by the reading's timeline. Stress will be minimal, and joy will abound
- **3 Fours** found in a Tarot layout indicate there is still contentment but perhaps a little more stress or work involved in maintaining your joy and serenity
- **2 Fours** laid out in a reading shows you are working towards a better balance in your life. You have increased focus but need to work to maintain it

If your reading has more than one 4 in it, then pay attention to your stability and focus. If a single 4 card is in the past position, then you are coming from a grounded place, building on that stability.

5
FIVES

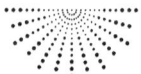

The Meaning of Multiple Fives

Five deals with power and control. It often appears in readings when struggles with power and control are dominating your life.

Take a look at yourself and the people you are engaging with at this moment in time. The power struggles could be an inner struggle with yourself and conflicting values. Or it could be in a relationship, either personal or professional. Ask yourself if you are being the dominate pushy one, or is someone attempting to control you? If it is you, can you change tactics, use your best communication skills and allow the other person, idea or topic room to be okay?

If the other person or business is pushing on you consider your options. Fives suggest that you use grace to try and change the situation. Ultimately, if you can't, you may need to remove yourself from the relationship.

Number 5 is the sephiroth called Geburah or Strength. It is also known as Severity. The judgement of God can be severe. Five asks that you use your strength in a positive way and let discipline guide your way.

If your Tarot layout has more than one 5 card, you are most definitely in a power struggle of some sorts. Again, is it you? Or is it the other person? Carefully consider what you are doing to irritate the situation. What is your role here? Have you lost control or perhaps repressed emotions that are now seeping out?

- **Four 5s** in a reading is significant. It may show a strong conflict or a major turning point in an issue you are working on. You are the middle of this, at this point. There is no clear resolution in sight, you must hang in there. For example, if this conflict is about a relationship, the relationship is not ending, but it is going through a tough time that might ultimately, lead to an end. Or the resolution will grow through the conflict and become stronger
- **Three 5s** appear in a reading when the universe is giving you a warning. The issue you are dealing with is about to become stronger and more difficult unless you can find a resolution now or a way to dial down the heat
- **Two fives** in a reading means defeat and trouble. It could mean you will lose something – your lover, a job, a contract. Heed the warning and make changes. Give yourself space from the issue so you can think with a clear head

Fives warns us to look at the energy of our life and our behaviour. It is a time consider our personalities and how they impact others. You may need healing in order to progress forward without anger.

6
SIXES

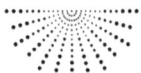

The Meaning of Multiple Sixes

Sixes resolve the conflict of 5's, moving you into harmony. Sixes indicate the journey to calmness. You are leaving disorder and upset to enter a time in your life where you can relax and take stock.

You may not be there – yet. You still may feel the lingering discord of an issue. Still, you see the way out, the path that will take to this new calmness. It is likely that you have even started down the path.

As the journey continues you will feel the weight of your concerns lift. A lightness will come. You see how all of the issues and concerns of your life can be resolved.

In Hebrew, six is the joining letter, and means 'hook'. It is a number of unity. Six is connection and completion. When six sides surround you (north, south, west, east, top and bottom), all is complete.

On the Tree of Life, Tiphereth (Beauty) is related to six. It represents love, family, harmony. Tiphereth is located midpoint on the Tree of Life. Where six is, there is affection and socializing.

- **Four 6s** show abundance is on its way. This is a positive sign

for relationships including financial relationships. You have much to look forward to in the next steps of your life
- **Three 6s** work almost as strongly as 4. It may take a little work on your part to receive the abundance. Remain open to the universe and accept what it brings you. You will be successful
- **Two 6s** tell you that whatever you are asking about is definitely a going concern. If it's a relationship, it will be good. If it's a job or a career move, the answer is a strong yes. Don't lose faith over any obstacles or minor irritations. See the goodness

7
SEVENS

The Meaning of Multiple Sevens

While 6 starts you on the journey to abundance and goodness, 7 delivers the goods. Seven brings you what you yearn for, your dreams begin to come true. There may still be a wait, but wait time is reduced from 6.

While 7 may bring you good things, it may sometimes seem as that it is not what you asked for. Relax and enjoy what the universe has brought you. Remember those times in life when you thought the worst had happened and suddenly life was great? You got fired from a job which motivated you to return to school. The person you were dating ended the relationship and it hurt. Until a few weeks later when you met your soul mate in a coffee shop. A dreaded move to a new city, gives you the shake-up you need, bringing forth your creativity. Sometimes things have to leave our lives in order to make room for the next step.

You didn't realize that what the universe delivered was exactly what you needed.

In Kabbalah teachings, the number 7 is perfection and completion.

Like 6, the 7th Sephiroth is Tiphereth (Beauty). Tiphereth is about balance, harmony and sensuality.

In Kabbalah the number seven symbolizes perfection. This is a natural perfection, not a manufactured one. Think of human beauty unaffected by plastic surgery. Seven is bringing the harmony and balance of Tipereth.

- **Four 7s** in your Tarot card reading is a sign that you are in a productive phase. There is ongoing potential surrounding you
- **Three 7s** appearing show you are working hard but need to put in more effort. It is time to listen to your gut and let the universe guide you.
- **Two 7s.** Take notice, for it is important when two 7s appear in answer to your question. Something is being created and it will be powerful if you put the energy in to nurture it

Seven's want you to follow your dreams. Don't put off chasing your goals. It is within reach. Six brought you calmness and now 7 shakes things up a bit. You've had enough rest, now you must work to reach your goal.

8
EIGHTS

The Meaning of Multiple Eights

Eight help you understand boundaries. Specifically, in the area of life you are seeking advice on from the Tarot. Eight is considered lucky or mystical in many cultures or religions. As such, any reading with an 8 in it is a positive omen.

Eights ask you to re-evaluate your life, your goals, relationships and values. Are you still on the right path? It is useful to re-evaluate on a regular basis so you can correct early if anything is out of balance.

The 8th Sephiroth is called Hod or Splendor. Eight is symbolic of life that is above nature and its limitations, moving into the spiritual realm. Eight is capable of much. As a double four, 8 is strength. It gives you new connections and openings. Hod is sincere and asks you to surround to the universe.

- **Four 8s** indicate a need to change paths. You've worked hard to achieve your goals but now you wonder if it was worth all the effort. Sometimes we reach for things that seem the right thing but as we approach success, we understand it was a fantasy. Something meant for others, not us. Or it was the

right thing when you started but life has changed, and it no longer suits who you've grown into. Now you are questioning if what you previously wanted is what you truly need
- It could also be that someone else choice this goal for you - society, a partner, a manager at work. You've come into your own. You realize that it isn't the path you are meant to walk
- **Three 8s** symbolize an offer to change to your life. But one that you don't take or only partially incorporate into your life. You continue on the path you are on, working towards your original goal. A good sign, all is good
- **Two Eights** are a sign of will-power and a determination to do the right thing

9
NINES

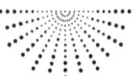

The Meaning of Multiple Nines

The number 9 points to drama. You're at the high point of drama, the final hurdle before the end and about to reach the end.

The 9th Sephiroth is known as Yesod (Foundation). Yesod is the reflection of everything. It gives the continuance of life and its energy. It is also creation. As in many things in the Tarot, if something ends, something else is beginning.

As Yesod contains everything, it has opposites within. Light and dark, yin and yang, your conscious thoughts and your unconscious leanings.

- **Four 9s** in a reading indicates movement. Something significant is going to happen within a situation in your life. Consider the question you or the seeker asked and look at the surrounding cards to discover in which area this will occur
- **Three 9s**, suggest a significant event will shortly occur in your life. This impact will be strong but not as deep as four

9s. You could be forced to move or have to change jobs. This impact doesn't have to be negative. You may initially view it as such, but hang on. It will turn into a positive
- **Two 9s** are telling you to be alert. To watch your world for the things the universe is presenting to you. Don't be so caught up in drama that you don't see the advantage of opportunities that are shown

10
TENS

The Meaning of Multiple Tens

Tens mark the beginning of newness. While 9 starts closing things off, 10 finishes the job but also shines light on new beginnings.

Malkuth (kingdom) is the 10th Sephiroth. It represents earth, nature and the blossoming of life. It tells you to be patient, your kingdom is coming. Life will be joyous. Use the strength of Malkuth to aid through any issues along the way.

- **Four 10s** in a Tarot card reading means you are likely finishing off projects. Or it may be a stage in life that is ending, giving you sorrow or sadness. But 10 is already creating newness, giving you a creative start to a new goal or purpose in life
- **Three 10s** symbolize similar endings and new beginnings. These endings are not as hard to let go of and will lead to newness fairly quickly. A relationship, a job or a project may be coming to a close but less painfully and the closure will move fast

- **Two 10s** laid out in a reading are also about endings and new beginnings. These endings are natural ones, like flowers dying in the fall. You're expecting this ending. Perhaps it was a short contract where you knew the end date. Or a vacation fling that you never intended to go the long haul. There is a tinge of sadness attached to the ending but already you are looking forward to the future

11
PAGES

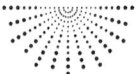

The Meaning of Multiple Pages

Pages are often young and energetic. They are the dreamers of the court cards. Pages are also messengers; they bring messages to you that others have not picked up on.

Pages are energetic and youthful, full of life. They are still developing their individuality and so come eagerly to each task, wondering if this is their life path. Pages love learning and gaining skills – so much that their enthusiasm can be overwhelming at times.

Pages invite you to use their energy to start new projects. You are at the beginning of a new life and they want you to embrace it lovingly and with an open mind.

- **Four Pages** in a Tarot reading indicate education is on the horizon. You may start a training course, an apprenticeship or go to university.
- Waite, the creator of the Rider Waite Tarot decks, believed that 4 Pages predicted illness
- **Three Pages** appearing in a reading, arguments may occur. There is a psychology concept which discusses triangles and

how difficult it can be for 3 people to get along when there is decision making involved. One person's feelings often get hurt. So 3 Pages may show that occurring in your life
- **Two Pages** mean that you have a youthful heart or perhaps are surrounded by youthful people who are strong in your life. Youth has little to do with age, it is an attitude. It is always good to have youthful energy enter your life

12
KNIGHTS

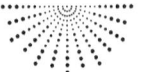

The Meaning of Multiple Knights

Tarot Knights are clever and ingenious. They love being in the middle of the action. The Knight has undertaken his journey and he wants to keep moving on the path.

Knights are more mature than Pages. They have experience, enough to guide them, but they don't have the wisdom or understanding that the Queens and Kings do. Sometime they go too slow, sometimes too fast. This can cause excess in both emotions and tasks. That excess can cause trouble.

- **Four Knights** in a reading means a possible struggle where you don't have the upper hand. Knights would indicate that the struggle occurs with young adults (20s, 30s) who are on their way to maturity and independence but haven't quite achieved it
- **Three Knights** suggests a lot of discussion will occur around you. Unlike 4 Knights, these discussions are not arguments, more debate like where ideas are exchanged

- **Two Knights** showing up in response to a question mean it is likely that you will have old friends or former romantic liaisons reappear in your life

13
QUEENS

The Meaning of Multiple Queens

Queens are commanding and powerful. They rule as strongly as Kings do and with the same authority.

Queens are mature and have a deep understanding of who they are and their role in the world. Her wisdom is dispensed in a nurturing manner as she works to allow others to fulfill their dreams. Queens don't need to be physically strong; her power comes from the inside. She is gentle and subtle. She quietly brings you into her plans, guiding you to the best path.

- **Four Queens** laid in a Tarot reading say you will be surrounded by powerful, independent women. Women who aren't afraid to express themselves or steer their way through life. Or, it could be that you are given the strength of 4 women to carry forward with your goals. You might attend a large group or network event. Generally, it bodes well for your career and relationships
- **Three Queens** appear when the universe is warning you to be wary of people around you. Male or female, someone

may be speaking negatively about you behind your back. You are being deceived in some way
- **Two Queens** give you support. There are people around you who care and are watching out for you. Depending on the question asked, this could be personal, or career related

14
KINGS

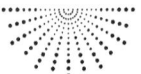

The Meaning of Multiple Kings

Kings are the most mature of the Court Cards. They are well-traveled, mature and successful.

Kings have emotional control. They are stable and well-balanced personalities. They know when to follow the flow and when to shift in order to reach their goals. Kings are responsible people. They like to take care of others while ensuring their own life is strong and has deep meaning.

Kings remind you to stand firm. Maintain your power without imposing on others.

- **Four Kings** in a reading give you a strong influence over any situation you are currently in. You could be promoted or working with powerful people who will have a positive influence on your life. If so, watch them carefully. You can model your behaviour after them and learn the positive ways to use your own power
- **Three Kings** appear in relation to a power situation. Check that you are not dominating, nor are being dominated by

your partner. The best relationships are those where the power shifts equally between those involved. In a career or other adventures, you will have support, but not as strong as 4 Kings. Again, be careful that you are not dominating, give others equal space for their opinions

- **Two Kings** gives you help and support from strong, influential people, but not as strong as receiving 3 or 4 Kings. It indicates a mentor or a partner who is both guiding and supporting you on an individual level

NOTES

1. THE FOOL ENCOUNTERS THE WORLD

1. Gray, Eden, *A Complete Guide To The Tarot*, (Bantam Book, New York), 1972, p.13
2. Gray, Eden, *A Complete Guide To The Tarot*, (Bantam Book, New York), 1972, p.11

1. THE FOOL

1. de, Laurence, *The Illustrated Key to the Tarot*, (The de Laurence Company, Chicago, Ill.) 1918 Section 2
2. The Master Theon, *The Book of Thoth*, (Samuel Weiser, Inc, New York) 1974, p.53

2. THE MAGICIAN

1. Wikipedia, *Hermes Trismegistus*, https://en.wikipedia.org/wiki/Hermes_Trismegistus

5. THE EMPEROR

1. Wikipedia, *Pythagoreanism*, https://en.wikipedia.org/wiki/Pythagoreanism

1. WANDS

1. Crowley, Aleister, *The Book of Toth*, (Samuel Weiser, Inc, New York) 1974, p.177

2. CUPS

1. Crowley, Aleister, *The Book of Toth*, (Samuel Weiser, Inc, New York) 1974, p.177

3. SWORDS

1. Crowley, Aleister, *The Book of Toth*, (Samuel Weiser, Inc, New York) 1974, p.177

4. PENTACLES

1. Crowley, Aleister, *The Book of Toth*, (Samuel Weiser, Inc, New York) 1974, p.177

ABOUT THE AUTHOR

Lydia Straub has been reading and studying Tarot cards for over 40 years. She's read cards for hundreds of people, using the Jungian psychology interpretation.

As a teacher and course designer, Lydia wants to share her knowledge with others. Creating and delivering the Tarot Instinct course is one of the joys of her life.

You can find her course on Udemy.com Tarot Instinct.